NATIONAL INVESTIGATORS' EXAMINATION

GENERAL PRINCIPLES, POLICE POWERS AND PROCEDURES

'There is nothing more deceptive than an obvious fact.'

Sir Arthur Conan Doyle

Anthony Turner
CITP, Cert Ed, BA (Hons) Ed, MA

Copyright © 2023 Anthony Turner All rights reserved

No part of this publication may be reproduced, distributed or transmitted in any form or by any means, including photocopying, recording or other electronic or mechanical methods without the prior written permission of the author except in the case of brief quotations embodied in reviews and certain other non-commercial uses permitted by copyright law.

ABOUT THE AUTHOR

Welcome to General Principles, Police Powers and Procedures which, in conjunction with Serious Crime, Property and Sexual Offences has been designed to help you successfully negotiate the National Investigators' Examination.

I joined the Metropolitan Police Service in 1981 before transferring to Hampshire Constabulary in 1986 where I spent the next fourteen years on the frontline before becoming a part time 'Devolved Trainer.'

With responsibility for providing localised training for officers and staff in new legislation, policy and procedures, I facilitated weekly training sessions for officers studying for promotion to the rank of Sergeant and Inspector. It therefore seemed sensible to have a go myself and thankfully I was successful in passing, at my first attempt, what was then referred to as OSPRE Part 1 (now NPPF Step 2: Legal Knowledge examination) along with the Part 2 assessment centre.

This ultimately led to an opening at Hampshire's Southern Support and Training HQ where, having become an accredited *Multiple Choice Question* writer, I created and facilitated a bespoke 'Study Programme and Refresher Course' designed to address a force wide shortage of officers qualified for promotion to the ranks of Sergeant and Inspector.

Extending this remit to include officers seeking to become detectives through the National Investigators' Examination, by the time I left the SS&T HQ as an Inspector, this shortfall had been addressed with percentage pass rates in the mid to high seventies.

Having retired in 2011, I, like so many others, adapted 30 years of learning in the job to a range of other ventures. That was until the advent of the coronavirus pandemic, during which I felt it was time to give something back to those of you who have kept us safe during those and ongoing difficult times.

The only question was, how?

In recognising the pressures each and every one of you face when seeking to manage your work life balance against the absolute need to study for this examination, in 2021 I published this series of annually updated, cost effective handbooks through Amazon KDP (Kindle Direct Publishing) which offer an easily digestible format focusing attention on those key areas of learning which regularly appear in the NIE.

In 2022, I took this one stage further by launching my YouTube channel:

@AnthonyTurner.NPPF-NIE

…where I have provided over **400 FREE 'Lead in and Two Option' QUESTIONS** to supplement the information and questions in the handbooks.

Finally, for 2023, the icing on the cake has been the publication of a mock exam, again through Amazon KDP, which I also hope you will find helpful in supporting your individual study programmes.

This is my way of saying 'thank you' and to wish you every success in the future.

Best wishes.

Tony

Anthony Turner
CTP, Cert Ed, BA(Hons) Ed, MA

CONTENTS

INTRODUCTION 7

KEY PRINCIPLES 9

SESSION 1
- Entry Search and Seizure 15

SESSION 2
- Detention and Treatment of Persons in Custody 29

SESSION 3
- Identification 69

SESSION 4
- Interviews 109

SESSION 5
- Release of Persons Arrested 131

SESSION 6
- Disclosure of Evidence 151

SESSION 7
- The Regulation of Investigatory Powers Act 2000 169

SESSION 8
- Court Procedure and Witnesses 181

INTRODUCTION

The National Investigators' Examination adopts a multiple choice question (MCQ) format which comes entirely from the *current* edition of the Blackstone's Police Investigators' Manual, so while there might be a temptation to buy an older copy from a colleague, personally I wouldn't on the basis that with questions derived from:

- Legislation
- Caselaw
- Keynotes

...the importance of being up to date in all such areas is evidenced by, for example, R v Ghosh (1982) which, up until recently, dealt with the subjective test of 'Dishonesty' under the Theft Act 1968.

This case was subsequently overruled by the Supreme Court in Ivey v Genting Casinos (2018) and Barton and Booth v R (2020) however, further clarification now states this test will be considered objectively in accordance with civil cases set out in Barlow Clowes International (in liq) v Eurotrust International Ltd [2006] and Royal Brunei Airlines Sdn v Tan [1995].

Consequently, the former rulings provide for excellent distractors when compiling an MCQ on this subject.

In terms of the questions themselves you'll be required to answer 80 MCQs in 2 hours which roughly equates to 90 seconds a question.

While this may sound a lot of time, trust me it isn't, especially if you spend too much time dithering on one question or fretting over another while trying to focus on the next. So, if you can learn to deal with this type of head blocker and move quickly on, then please do so or you'll waste valuable time. It is an art, but one well worth getting to grips with and most importantly comes with practice.

Of the 80 MCQs, 10 of those which have performed least well in the exam will be removed from the marking process, thus ensuring candidates are not unfairly penalised.

The pass mark is in turn set in stone at 55.7% which requires 37 of the 70 questions to be answered correctly.

Further information on these subjects can be found on-line at the College of Policing website which I urge you to study carefully to ensure you have a full appreciation of what is required, not just for the examinations themselves, but also for the extraneous issues surrounding this examination process.

Finally, while every effort has been made to ensure this handbook accurately reflects legislation, caselaw, statistical analysis and questions, neither the author nor publisher are held responsible for the results accrued from the advice in this book.

KEY PRINCIPLES

So before we get started let's take a look at some of the key principles surrounding MCQ writing along with some *hints and tips* which will help you maximise the time available for each question.

Referred to as 'A' Type questions the MCQs exclusively consist of:

- a 'Stem,' which includes a case, scenario or vignette (that's a posh word for setting the scene);
- a 'Lead in,' which specifies the question to which you're asked to provide an answer;
- and four options of which one is obviously correct while the other three are plausible distractors, hence the earlier R v Ghosh analogy.

Each MCQ will range from 55 to 250 words, in theory allowing for a 50:50 split between reading and decision time, for example...

QUESTION

While on patrol in the High Street at 3 a.m. Police Constables GILLARD and KIMBER approach three youths who are in possession of unlit petrol bombs. The youths scatter and throw the bombs away before they are detained and arrested by the officers for the offence of affray.

In accordance with Section 3 of the Public Order Act 1986 (Affray) have the officers acted correctly under these circumstances?

A. Yes, as the conduct of the youths would cause a person of reasonable firmness present to fear for his/her personal safety.
B. Yes, as mere possession of the petrol bombs would constitute a threat for the purpose of this offence.
C. No, for this offence to be complete the conduct of the youths must be directed towards property.
D. No, for this offence to be complete the conduct of the youths must be directed towards a person present at the scene.

The answer to this question combines the definition of the offence of affray with caselaw as follows.

Definition
- A person is guilty of affray if he uses or threatens unlawful violence towards another and his conduct is such as would cause a person of reasonable firmness present at the scene to fear for his personal safety.

Caselaw
- Answer 'A' is incorrect on the basis that while R v Sanchez (1996) & R v Carey (2006) identifies that 'a person of reasonable firmness' does not have to be present at the scene, I v DPP 2001 clarifies that in order to prove the offence of affray, the threat of unlawful violence must be directed towards a person present.
- Answer 'B' is also incorrect as while possession of the petrol bombs would constitute a threat, the conduct must still be directed 'towards another.'
- Likewise answer 'C' is incorrect as unlawful violence is again restricted by the term 'towards another' and does not include property.
- Answer 'D' is therefore correct based on the House of Lords ruling that, in order to prove the offence of affray, the threat of unlawful violence must be directed towards a person present (I v DPP 2001).

So bearing in mind the average time for each question is 90 seconds, you may find the following suggestions useful...

READ THE QUESTION
- Sounds obvious, but you may be surprised how many candidates think they *'know what the question is about'* and skip over important information in the 'Stem' and choose a credible yet incorrect option.

COVER UP
- Answering the question in your mind before looking at the four options will save time when reviewing the answers, but only if you're sure of your facts, for example...

QUESTION

DC GOTTEN wishes to carry out non-urgent directed surveillance on a commercial car repair garage belonging to LEWES. It is suspected that LEWES is operating a car-ringing enterprise at the garage and DC GOTTEN wishes to obtain intelligence about the alleged offence.

Who can authorise this surveillance and for how long?

A. An officer of the rank of inspector or above may authorise this surveillance for a period up to 3 months.
B. An officer of the rank of inspector or above may authorise this surveillance for a period up to 6 months.
C. An officer of the rank of superintendent or above may authorise this surveillance for a period up to 3 months.
D. An officer of the rank of superintendent or above may authorise this surveillance for period up to 6 months.

By knowing even one element of the answer before looking, in this instance you're already half way to answering the question which, in the case is C.

KEY WORDS

- Recognising key words in definitions may also help you focus on the correct answer however, on occasions they can also be confusing for example...

QUESTION

EALES rents a house under a **tenancy** agreement from his local council. EALES is short of money and decides to sell off several items from the house to help him through a cash crisis.

Which of the following circumstances is correct when dealing with the offence of **theft of land** in accordance with section 4(2) Theft Act 1968?

A. EALES **picks** flowers from the front garden to sell at a car boot sale and may commit the offence of theft of land.

B. EALES **severs** some topsoil from the garden to sell to his neighbour and may commit the offence of theft of land.
C. EALES **removes a fireplace** to sell at a nearby second-hand shop and may commit the offence of theft of land.
D. EALES cannot commit the offence of theft of land while under a **tenancy agreement**.

So once you've focused on the *tenancy* element in the stem of the question and the *removal of a fireplace* in the options, you'll know C is your correct answer.

ELIMINATION

- Even though you may not be 100% sure of the answer, eliminating the clearly incorrect options can still achieve a positive result.

LEAD IN

- By reading the 'Lead In' FIRST, you'll be aware of what information is required from the 'Stem' e.g. the type of offence. Good for some questions but not all, for example...

QUESTION

GILCHRIST has just started a new job at a bank when she is approached by BAXTER who tells her that he knows she used to be a prostitute and that if she does not have sexual intercourse with his friend, HUMPHRIES, he will inform the bank manager and she will probably be sacked. GILCHRIST reluctantly agrees to BAXTER's demand and has sexual intercourse with HUMPHRIES.

Is this an offence of Blackmail contrary to section 21 of the Theft Act 1968?

A. Yes, because BAXTER makes the unwarranted demand with a view to gain a benefit for another.
B. No, because gain for the purposes of this offence extends only to the obtaining of money or other property.
C. Yes, because gain for the purposes of this offence relates to anything including sexual gratification.

D. No, because BAXTER did not make the demand with a view to gain for himself.

Answer B HOWEVER, as mentioned, this is not always the case.

QUESTION

TURVEY has just lost his job and is finding money hard to come by. RANDELL feels sorry for him and gives TURVEY a packet of ten cigarettes that also contains a small amount of cocaine. TURVEY knows nothing about the cocaine inside the packet of cigarettes. Several hours later, TURVEY is stopped by Police Constable MAIR, who discovers the cocaine inside the cigarette packet.

Which of the following statements is correct with regard to TURVEY?

A. As TURVEY has physical control of the cigarettes and knows of their presence he also has 'possession' of the drug.
B. The only requirement for 'possession' is that TURVEY had the drug in his physical control.
C. To show that TURVEY has 'possession' of the drug you must show that he actually knew what he possessed was cocaine.
D. TURVEY cannot be in 'possession' of the cocaine because he does not know of its existence.

Answer A.

Ultimately, while MCQs are derived from anywhere within the Blackstone's Police Investigators' Manual, their primary focus is quite rightly on operational areas of policing.

With that in mind, you'll find the handbooks include a variety of 'A' style questions along with a host of other single answer options and my personal favourite which, if you've done your homework, are short, sharp and punchy questions with 2 head scratching options you'll invariably be left pondering over in the exam.

So, with all that in mind, let's get started.

GENERAL PRINCIPLES
POLICE POWERS & PROCEDURES

SESSION 1

ENTRY, SEARCH AND SEIZURE

Search Warrants s.8 PACE
'Indictable Offences'

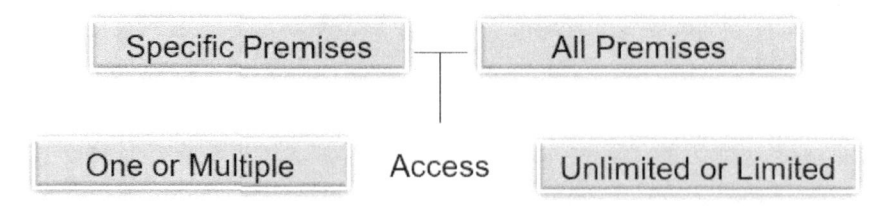

```
    Specific Premises  ──┬──  All Premises
                         │
   One or Multiple     Access    Unlimited or Limited
```

RGB material sought is likely be of **substantial value to the investigation** and **relevant evidence**

It does not authorise seizure of all material found but allows for a preliminary sift of material on site before removal

> Intelligence Material

Note
- A constable can apply for 2 different types of warrant under S8 PACE:
    - **Specific premises** i.e. to search one set of premises occupied or controlled by an individual;
    - **All premises** i.e. when it is necessary to search all premises occupied or controlled by an individual, but where it is not reasonably practicable to specify all such premises at the time of applying.
    - In both instances, the warrant *may* authorise access on more than one occasion.
    - Multiple entry warrants may be unlimited or limited to a maximum number.
- The justice of the peace must, in addition to the officer applying, also have RGB an indictable offence has been committed, along with RGB that the material sought is likely to be of substantial value to the investigation and relevant evidence.

R v Chief Constable of the Warwickshire Constabulary ex parte Fitzpatrick (1999)
- Where there are RGB material is likely to be of substantial value etc, the material seized by the officer must be shown to have fallen within this criteria.

Relevant Evidence
- Means anything admissible in evidence at a trial.

R v Chesterfield, ex parte Bramley 2000
- While a s.8 warrant provides for a preliminary sift of material it does NOT allow seizure of ALL material to be taken away and sifted elsewhere.

Intelligence Material
- Material which is **solely** for **intelligence** purposes may **not** be seized under Section 8.

WARRANT APPLICATION / EXECUTION
Entry & Search s.15 / 16 PACE

Where a constable applies for such a warrant it shall be his duty to

STATE

Grounds   Premises   Enactment

IDENTIFY
Articles or Persons Sought

Ex Parte

Information in Writing

Grounds
- On which he makes the application.

Enactment
- Legislation under which the warrant would be issued e.g. Theft Act.

Premises
- Which is desired to enter and search and includes:
    - Vehicles / Vessels / Hovercraft / Offshore and Renewable Energy Installations;
    - Tents / Moveable Structures.

Articles
- So far as is practicable.

Ex Parte
- Means the warrant shall be applied for without the recipient's knowledge \ presence & supported by *information in writing*.

Additionally
- Name of *Applicant*.
- *Date* of Issue.

Authorising Officer
- Inspector or above, however, in cases of urgency, where no such officer is readily available the *senior officer* on duty.
- Superintendent or above for terrorism related applications.

Q. How many copies?
A. Two (2) certified as copies.

Q. Within what period of time?
A. Three (3) months from the dates of issue so not the date of application.

Q. What part of the day?
A. Reasonable time unless it will frustrate purpose of the search.

Q. What if not in uniform?
A. Show documentary evidence that a constable (warrant card).

Q. What if the person is not in?
A. Normally give one of the two (2) copies to the person, but in this instance leave in a prominent place on the premises, unless someone else is present who appears to the constable to be in charge of the premises.

Q. Can the warrant authorise other people to accompany the officer?
A. Yes, although some warrants *require* the presence of another e.g. under S135 MHA.

Q. Will minor departures from the letter of the warrant render the search unlawful?
A. No, but note the word *minor*.

Q What happens to the warrant after execution or non use?
A. Return to an 'Appropriate Person:'
- If issued by a Justice of the Peace = Designated Officer;
- If issued by a Judge = Appropriate Officer of the Court from which it was issued.

Q. How many times can the warrant be executed?
A. Once, unless it specifies multiple occasions.

Q. If an application is refused, can further applications be made?
A. Yes, subject to being supported by additional grounds.

QUESTION

Detective Constable COLE and her colleagues are executing an 'All Premises' warrant at a property occupied by JAKEWAY, when she discovers a document which shows JAKEWAY has control of a previously unknown lock up nearby. DC COLE has reasonable grounds to believe property of substantive value to the investigation may be found in this lock up however, she is unsure what she should do next.

In relation to section 16(3A) PACE 1984 which of the following statements is correct?

A. DC COLE must obtain written authorisation from a senior officer to search this lock up.
B. DC COLE must obtain written authorisation from an Inspector or above to search this lock up.
C. DC COLE must obtain a further 'Specified Premises' warrant from a Justice of the Peace for this lockup.
D. DC COLE must obtain a further 'Specified Premises' warrant from a Judge for this lock up.

Answer B.

Although in cases of urgency, applications for all search warrants may be authorised by a senior officer on duty where an Inspector or above is not 'readily available,' this does not extend to this type of situation under section 16(3A), so *A is incorrect.*

Bearing in mind the impracticality of obtaining a further warrant from either a JP or Judge under these circumstances, thankfully *C and D are also incorrect.*

So, when dealing with an 'All Premises' warrant and, as in this case, further information comes to light regarding another property *not shown* on the original application i.e. the lock up which is also occupied or controlled by the individual, then any subsequent requirement to search these premises must be authorised in writing by an Inspector or above.

Similarly, section 16(3B) goes onto say that for ALL Multiple Authorisation warrants, no premises may be entered or searched for the second or any subsequent occasion, again without the written authorisation from an Inspector or above.

Power of Entry
s.17 PACE

A constable may enter and search any premises for the following purposes

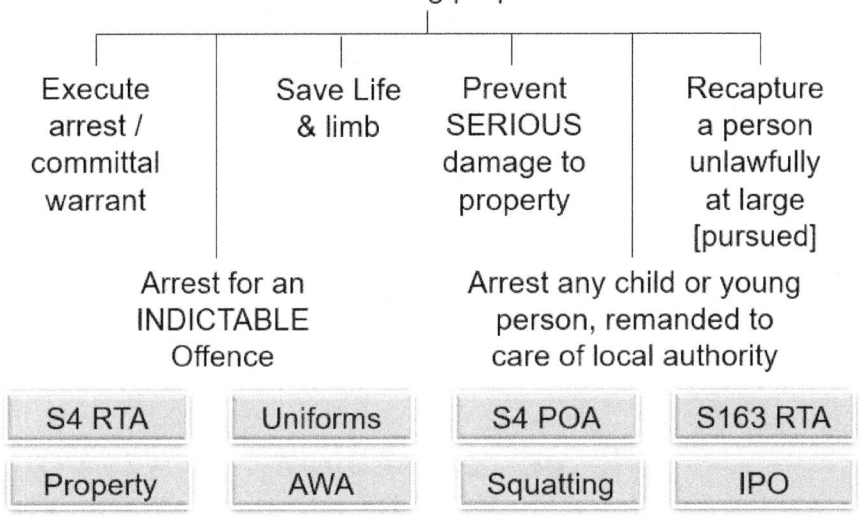

- Execute arrest / committal warrant
- Save Life & limb
- Prevent SERIOUS damage to property
- Recapture a person unlawfully at large [pursued]

Arrest for an INDICTABLE Offence

Arrest any child or young person, remanded to care of local authority

S4 RTA	Uniforms	S4 POA	S163 RTA
Property	AWA	Squatting	IPO

Note
- Designated persons e.g. PCSO's/CSOs *if specifically authorised* may also enter in order to *save life & limb OR prevent serious damage to property*.
- In the MAJORITY of instances the officer must have RGB that the person is on the premises so mere suspicion is not enough EXCEPT for *saving life and limb*.

Unlawfully at large
- Can apply to someone who has escaped from custody and is being pursued aka *'hot pursuit.'*

HOWEVER

- For someone subject to an order under the Mental Health Act where the order requires them to be returned to hospital, the term used for the pursuit is *'almost contemporaneous.'*

Powers of arrest:
- **S4 RTA** unfit through drink or drugs;
- **Uniform** prohibition of uniforms s.1 Public Order Act;
- **Property** offences of entering and remaining on property e.g. violence to secure entry [Criminal Law Act]
- **S4 POA** fear or provocation of violence;
- **s.163 RTA 1988** failure to stop when required by a constable in uniform;
- **IPO** failing to comply with an interim possession order;
- **AWA** offences relating to prevention of cruelty to animals under the Animal Welfare Act 2006;
- **Squatting** in a *residential* building under the Legal Aid, Sentencing and Punishment of Offenders Act 2012.

Inspectors authority
s.18 PACE

An Inspector may authorise a constable, in writing, to enter & search any premises

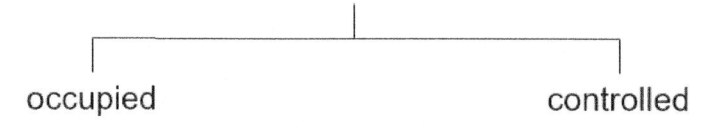

- occupied
- controlled

by a person who is under arrest for an INDICTABLE offence if he has reasonable grounds for SUSPECTING that there is evidence on the premises of

- that offence
- another Indictable offence

connected with or similar to that offence

Note
- A constable may conduct a S18 search without the permission of the Inspector IF before taking the detained person to the police station *his/her presence is necessary for the effective investigation of the offence.*
- The Inspector MUST however be informed asap after the search.
- Details of the search must be recorded in the custody record.
- If a detained person is re-arrested for an indictable offence the powers under s.18 begin again.

QUESTION

Where it has been *necessary for the effective investigation of the offence* for a s.18 search to be conducted prior to arrival at the police station, which of the following must be retrospectively recorded in writing by the inspector?

A. Grounds and nature of the evidence sought.
B. Grounds and nature of the evidence found.

Answer A.

QUESTION

Constable JENKINS is seeking an Inspector's authority in relation to searching a bedsit which he suspects is occupied by GRANT, who is in custody on suspicion of Burglary, an indictable offence.

In respect of these circumstances, is the Inspector able to authorise the search of GRANT's bedsit?

A. Yes, the search may be authorised as it is suspected that GRANT occupies or controls the bedsit.
B. Yes, as GRANT is in custody on suspicion of having committed an indictable offence the request may be authorised.
C. No, the search may not be authorised unless it is believed that GRANT occupies or controls the bedsit.

D. No, the search may not be authorised unless GRANT actually occupies or controls the bedsit.

Answer D.

It is a factual requirement that the premises are occupied or controlled. An officer's suspicion or belief is insufficient HOWEVER a short stay MAY amount to 'occupation' the extent of which being able to support the belief that the occupation WILL have *caused or contributed* to the evidence being on the premises.

Lineham v DPP (2000)
- Where officers failed to explain or attempt to explain to an occupier the reason for the entry and search this may result in them not acting in the course of their duty and render any subsequent resistance on the part of the occupier lawful.

Search upon Arrest
S. 32 PACE

A constable may search an arrested person if he has RGB he may be a danger to himself or others or for anything which

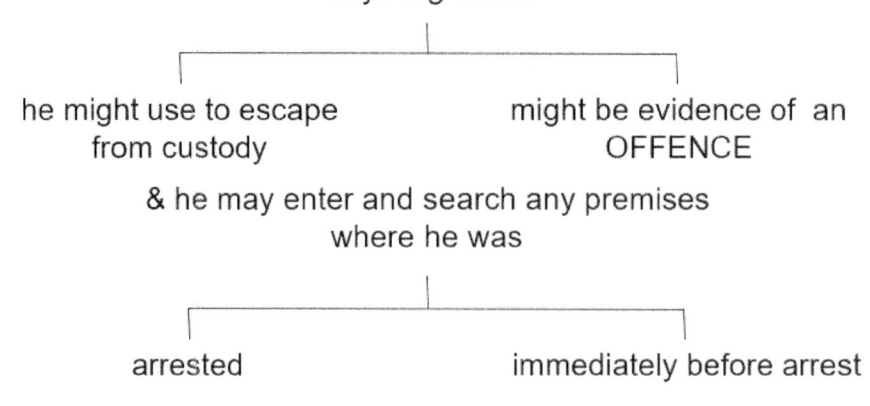

- he might use to escape from custody
- might be evidence of an OFFENCE

& he may enter and search any premises where he was

- arrested
- immediately before arrest

for evidence of the INDICTABLE offence for which he was arrested

Note
The key to s.32 is that it must be viewed in 2 parts:
1. The first section is about searching the arrested *person* in connection with *any offence* e.g. public order, TWOC, Burglary etc;
2. The second is about searching the *premises* in connection with the *indictable* offence for which the person has been arrested so forget the public order, TWOC etc, but stick with the Burglary.

R v Badham (1987)
- This power should only be used at the time of the arrest and not to return to the premises later in the day when perhaps a s.18 power to search may be appropriate.

Arrested Person
- Is a person who has been arrested *other than at a police station*.
- If at the police station then we would be using the common law power to search for anything to harm self, escape etc and also if in the custody centre, s.18 for any subsequent search of premises.

Search for evidence of an offence
- Does not include the removal of clothing in a public place other than his outer coat, jacket & gloves i.e. as in S1 PACE BUT it does extend this authorisation to include a search of a persons mouth.

Extent of the search
- To that which is reasonably required.
- If your looking for a car engine to go looking in kitchen cupboards would not be appropriate HOWEVER evidence of documentation relating to the offence may be applicable dependent on the circumstances.

Multi-occupied premises
- The arrested persons room and other communal areas e.g. kitchen, lounge etc but not another resident's room.

QUESTION

Police Constable DEAR has just arrested SALISBURY on suspicion of an offence of Burglary. SALISBURY had just left the front door of a friend's house, having been inside for some hours. Constable DEAR now wishes to search the house.

Considering ONLY Section 32 of PACE 1984, which of the following is true in relation to the search of the house?

A. PC DEAR must reasonably suspect that there is evidence on the premises relating to the Burglary.
B. PC DEAR must genuinely believe that there is evidence on the premises relating to the Burglary.
C. PC DEAR must reasonably suspect that there is evidence on the premises relating to an offence.
D. PC DEAR must genuinely believe that there is evidence on the premises relating to an offence.

Answer B.

HOWEVER

Hewitson v Chief Constable of Dorset Police (2003)
- Divisional Court refused to allow a s.32 to be used where the arrested person had NOT been in the relevant premises (where he did not live) for a period of 2 hours prior to his arrest AND this includes where there were NO RGB he presented a danger to self or others.
- In other words, if the officers wanted to search the individual they would have to rely on another power e.g. s.1 PACE if the circumstances allowed.

General Power of Seizure
S.19 PACE

When lawfully on premises and a constable has reasonable grounds for BELIEVING that property

- has been obtained in consequence of the commission of an offence
- is evidence in relation to an offence

&

seizure is necessary to prevent the property being

Concealed   Altered   Destroyed

Lost   Damaged

Lawfully on Premises
- Can be withdrawn, so once they are told to leave that's it, end of power.
- This applies even though the officers may be given a reasonable time to leave, so they cannot seize property if for example they spot it on the way out of the door.

HOWEVER

- Don't forget there are other powers available if the person is arrested, so read the lead in carefully and make sure you know what is being asked of you.

Cowan v Commissioner of Police for the Metropolis (2000)
- Identifies that premises include vehicles and that this power of seizure extends to premises so the vehicle can be seized.

Wood v North Avon Magistrates' Court (2009)
- While the power extends to seizure of vehicles or other items such as tents, caravans so they can taken to a police station to preserve evidence, this only applies to items on the premises so not for example a car parked in a car park adjacent to the premises.

Intelligence purposes.
- This power does NOT extend to seizure of property solely for intelligence purposes.

QUESTION

Where information is stored in an electronic form and is accessible from the premises, which of the following statements is correct?

A. A constable may require the information to be provided in a form that is visible and legible where he/she has reasonable grounds for believing that it is evidence in relation to *the offence being investigated.*

B. A constable may require the information to be provided in a form that is visible and legible where he/she has reasonable grounds for believing that it is evidence in relation to *the offence being investigated or any other offence.*

Answer B. A constable may require the information to be provided in a form that is visible and legible where he/she has reasonable grounds for believing that it is evidence in relation to *the offence being investigated or any other offence* OR it has been obtained in consequence of an offence AND seizure is necessary to prevent it being concealed, lost or destroyed.

Retention of seized material
- Will apply unless a photograph or copy would suffice SO the original is not absolutely necessary.
- Car key seized from a drunk driver MUST be returned on release from custody.

GENERAL PRINCIPLES
POLICE POWERS & PROCEDURES

SESSION 2

DETENTION AND TREATMENT OF PERSONS BY POLICE OFFICERS

Custody Officer at Police Stations

Designated	Non Designated
Designated custody officer who must be a sergeant	Any officer not involved in the investigation of the offence
⬇	⬇
Sergeant not involved in the investigation of the offence	The arresting officer where no other officer is available
⬇	⬇
Any officer not involved in the investigation of the offence	Any other officer involved in the investigation

In the event a detained person is taken to or released on bail prior to arrival at a non designated station the officer, who acts as a custody officer, must inform an Inspector at a designated police station

Vince v Chief Constable of Dorset (1993)
- The Chief Constable (CC) is under a duty (must) to appoint one custody officer (CO) for each designated station while having a discretionary power (may) to appoint more than one.

PACE s.36(3) &(4)
- The CO must be an officer of *at least* the rank of sergeant however, officers of any rank may perform this duty if an officer of that rank is not available.

Q. Where a patrol sergeant is on duty at the time a DP is brought into custody, will this officer be required to step in and perform the functions of a custody sergeant in favour of 'Any Officer?'
A. Yes, subject to the provision of operational requirements.
B. No, on the basis that the patrol sergeant has another *role to perform*
Answer B. However, were this not to be the case, then 'Any Officer' performing this duty *will* be unlawful.

Note
- PACE requires a person to be taken to a police station *as soon as reasonably practicable* after arrest unless otherwise bailed prior to arrival.

HOWEVER

- Not all police stations have charge rooms or facilities for dealing with a detained person (DP) and as such PACE also states that where a DP is to be detained or likely to be detained for *more than 6 hours* then they must go to a designated police station.
- The Police Station may be designated for *whole days only,* not for part days.

At a Police Station
- This phrase is defined as within the boundary of any building or enclosed yard that forms part of the Police Station and is of particular importance when considering issues surrounding the 'Relevant Time' of an detained person arriving at a police station, which we will come to a little later…

Insufficient Evidence to Charge

Where a custody officer considers there is insufficient evidence to charge a person, that person **must be released**

↓

unless there are **reasonable grounds for believing** that the person's detention is necessary to

SECURE or PRESERVE evidence relating to an offence for which the person has been arrested	or obtain such **EVIDENCE** by **QUESTIONING** the detained person

Note
- Believing not suspecting i.e. requires a greater amount of evidence than suspicion.

Will an interview be necessary in order to secure a charge?
- Not in all cases however, where *intent* or *dishonesty* is involved then in such circumstances questioning of a detained person MAY be necessary.

Written record
- A written record showing grounds for detention should be completed in the presence of the DP where it is practicable to do so. Where it is not practicable is listed as the person is:
    - Incapable of understanding;
    - Violent or likely to become violent;
    - In *urgent* need of medical attention.

Rights
- Rights including a solicitor MUST be offered regardless of whether the DP is being held incommunicado.

- CO should also ask *why* if refused and record reason on the custody record.

Fayed v Metropolitan Police Commissioner (2004)
- There is no express or implied requirement on a CO to enquire into the legality of the arrest & the CO is entitled to assume the arrest was lawful.
- Having said that if the CO is aware the arrest is unlawful HRA would make life difficult when defending their decision to detain the person.

The Stages of Detention
Authorisation Levels

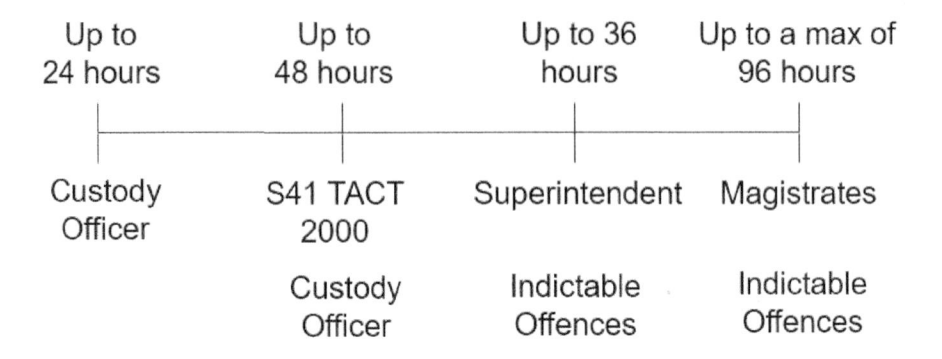

Up to 24 hours	Up to 48 hours	Up to 36 hours	Up to a max of 96 hours
Custody Officer	S41 TACT 2000 Custody Officer	Superintendent Indictable Offences	Magistrates Indictable Offences

Note
- The stages of detention commence from the *Relevant Time* which is the time of arrival at the police station so NOT the time at which the detained person is presented to the custody officer.

Up to a max of 96hrs
- First application will be for an additional **36hrs** followed by further applications up to the max of 96hrs.

Section 41 TACT
- Period of extension can be increased to a *maximum of 14 days* in *7 day periods* on application to a *District Judge at Magistrates Court* (so not a normal Magistrate) by a Supt or Crown Prosecutor.

QUESTION

CORNELL is arrested on suspicion of rape on Saturday at 1600 hours and taken to the local police station, arriving at 1630 hours. At 1800 hours CORNELL complains of feeling unwell and is taken to hospital, leaving the station at 1830 hours. After treatment, he arrives back at the station at 2300 hours.

At what time will the first stage of detention expire?

A. 1600 hours on Sunday.
B. 2100 hours on Sunday.
C. 2200 hours on Sunday.
D. 2300 hours on Sunday.

Answer B.

Having arrived at the police station at 1630hrs the relevant time for the first stage of detention (24 hrs) begins however travelling time to and from and while at hospital does not count. The clock therefore stops at 1830hrs (2 hrs into the relevant time period) and only resumes again at 2300 hrs when he returns to the police station. So with another 22 hours left on the clock, that takes us through to 2100hrs on Sunday.

Extension 24 to 36 hours

The Superintendent must be responsible for the station at which the person is detained

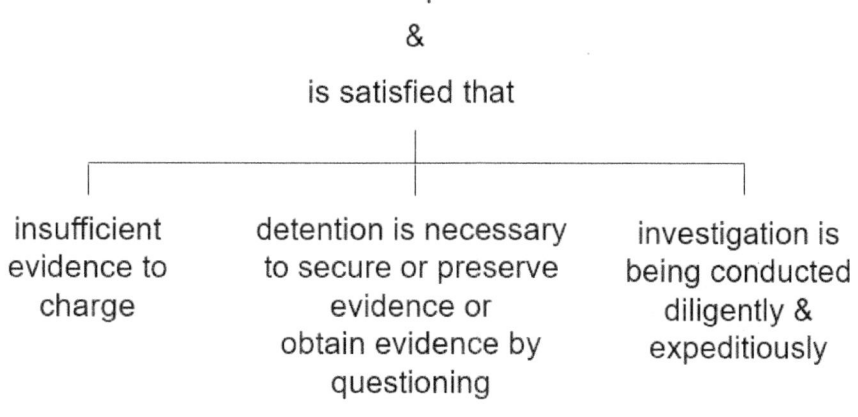

&

is satisfied that

| insufficient evidence to charge | detention is necessary to secure or preserve evidence or obtain evidence by questioning | investigation is being conducted diligently & expeditiously |

Note.
- Insufficient evidence to charge means that if there is *sufficient* evidence to charge then the extension cannot be authorised.
- The extension must be made within 24 hours of the relevant time and *cannot* be made before at least 2 Reviews have been carried out. It can however be made either *in person* or by *livelink*.

- This extension will *not* automatically become a review i.e. they are 2 distinct roles, although they can be done at the same time.

Magistrates grounds for extension
These are the same as for a superintendent and a *warrant* will be issued:
- Both the Police & the DP must be present, unless the Court gives direction for the hearing to be held by livelink;
- Initially, the magistrate's can issue a warrant for a further 36 hours and then extend this on further applications up to 96 hours;
- Applications may be made within the 36 hour period however where it is shown not to be practicable for the court to sit in that time then the laying of information may take place *within the next 6 hours*;
- Applications for the warrant can be made at anytime *even before a Superintendent review has been conducted*;

HOWEVER

- Once refused, no further applications may be made so the benefit of an early application must be considered carefully;
- In *Terrorism* cases the application must be made by a *Superintendent or Crown Prosecutor*.

QUESTION

GRIEVE has been arrested on suspicion of a Theft. After being in Police detention for 12 hours it is decided that there is insufficient evidence to charge him. He is released without charge. Subsequently, further evidence comes to light implicating him in the offence and GRIEVE is re-arrested.

Given these circumstances, what is the time limit for GRIEVE's detention?

A. 12 hours.
B. 24 hours.
C. 36 hours.
D. 48 hours.

Answer B.

The 24 hours starts again if a person has been released without charge i.e. NOT bailed to return to the Police station pending further enquiries.

QUESTION

Detective Sergeant CABLE is interviewing REGIS in relation to a Rape. REGIS' detention has already been authorised by a Superintendent up to the maximum permissible 36 hours. Detective Sergeant CABLE requires more time in which to question REGIS and therefore a magistrates court warrant must be applied for.

Who may apply for a Warrant of further detention?

A. Any rank.
B. Sergeant.
C. Inspector.
D. Superintendent.

Answer A.

Relevant Times

OPTION 1

If the suspect is arrested in
↓
Hampshire
↓
for an offence in
Hampshire

> the relevant time clock begins on arrival at the **FIRST** police station in Hampshire

Note
- On a normal day to day arrest in your own force area, the Relevant Time for a DP's *initial period of detention* begins at the time of arrival at your custody centre, so NOT at the time the DP's detention is authorised by the custody officer.
- There are however, some variations on this theme which relate to the suspect being arrested outside of your force area and the need for some travelling time before the relevant time clock begins.
- To this end and dependent on the circumstances, PACE factors in the need for UP TO *24 hours travelling time* when a suspect is detained out of your force area.
- This *24 hours travelling time* is NOT to be confused with the initial period of detention of 24 hours.

OPTION 2

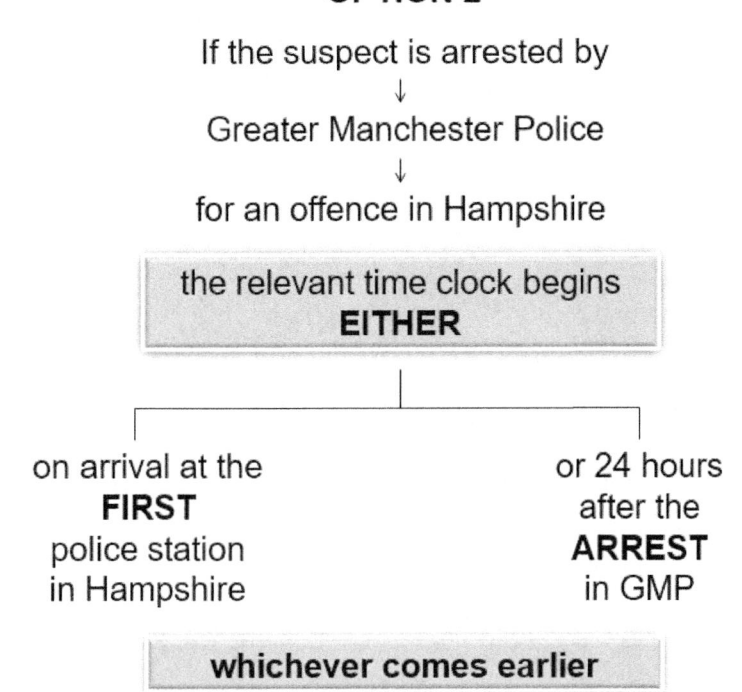

If the suspect is arrested by
↓
Greater Manchester Police
↓
for an offence in Hampshire

the relevant time clock begins
EITHER

on arrival at the **FIRST** police station in Hampshire

or 24 hours after the **ARREST** in GMP

whichever comes earlier

QUESTION

As a result of a PNC check, JONES is arrested in Manchester at 1400 hours on Monday for an offence committed in Portsmouth (Hampshire). The arresting officer informs Portsmouth of the arrest at 1500 hours and asks for an escort to be sent. The escort arrive in Manchester late that evening and stops overnight. They leave Manchester at 1000 hours on Tuesday and arrive at Portsmouth Central police station at 1530 hours on Tuesday.

When does JONES's relevant time begin?

A. 1400 hours on Monday.
B. 1500 hours on Monday.
C. 1400 hours Tuesday.
D. 1530 hours Tuesday.

Answer C. 1400 hours on Tuesday.

The relevant time begins *either* at the time of arrival at the first Police Station in the Police Area in which JONES is wanted *or* 24 hours after arrest, whichever is the *earlier*. In this case, JONES arrived at Portsmouth at 1530 hrs, 25 and a half hours after arrest. Therefore, the relevant time begins at 1400hrs i.e. 24 hours after Jones' time of arrest.

OPTION 3

If the suspect is arrested by
↓
West Yorkshire Police for an offence in Leeds
↓
BUT is also wanted for an offence in Hampshire

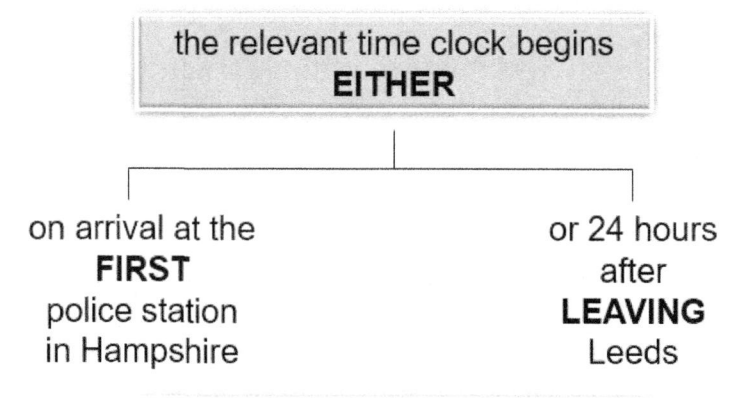

the relevant time clock begins
EITHER

on arrival at the **FIRST** police station in Hampshire

or 24 hours after **LEAVING** Leeds

whichever comes earlier

QUESTION

COX is arrested in Leeds for Burglary at 1600 hours on Tuesday and is being dealt with for the offence. A check reveals he is wanted in Basingstoke (Hampshire) for an offence of fraud. An escort from Basingstoke arrive in Leeds at 1200 hours on Wednesday as COX is being bailed. COX is arrested and the escort leave Leeds Central police station at 1300 hours. Owing to severe weather conditions, however, they have to stop overnight in London and the escort arrives at Basingstoke police station at 1100 hours on Thursday.

When does COX's relevant time begin?

A. 1200 hours on Wednesday.
B. 1600 hours on Wednesday.
C. 1100 hours on Thursday.
D. 1300 hours on Thursday.

Answer C. 1100 hrs on Thursday.

The relevant time begins *either* at the time of arrival at the first Police Station in the Police area that COX is wanted or 24 hours after the escort leaves the place at which he was first detained, whichever is the *earlier*. On this occasion, COX arrives at Basingstoke at 1100 hrs, 22 hours *after the escort left Leeds*. Therefore, the relevant time begins at 1100hrs.

OPTION 4

If the suspect is arrested outside
↓
England and Wales
↓
for an offence in Hampshire

> the relevant time clock begins
> **EITHER**

on arrival at the
FIRST
police station
in Hampshire

or 24 hours
after
ENTRY
into England

> whichever comes earlier

QUESTION

SMITH is extradited from Sweden and is due to arrive at Bristol airport at 2100 hours on Sunday night, however adverse weather conditions result in the aircraft being diverted to Edinburgh where it lands at 1930 hours. The escort stay overnight in Edinburgh and continue their journey on Monday leaving Edinburgh police station at 1000 hours crossing into England at 1200 hours. They arrive at Southampton Central police station (Hampshire) at 2000 hours on Monday.

When does SMITH's relevant time begin?

A. 1930 hours on Monday.
B. 2000 hours on Monday.
C. 1000 hours on Tuesday.
D. 1200 hours on Tuesday.

Answer B. 2000hrs Monday.

The relevant time begins *either* at the time of the detained person's arrival at the first Police station in England and Wales OR 24 hours after his/her entry into England and Wales, whichever is the *earlier*. In this case, the arrival at Southampton Police Station was only 8 hours after entering England.

The first police station
- Remember, the clock starts ticking when the DP arrives at the 1st Police Station in the force where the suspect is wanted.
- So don't stop off for a cup of tea, for example in Andover (Hampshire) on the way to Portsmouth (Hampshire) or the clock will start once you get to Andover not Portsmouth.
- Also, don't forget that the phrase 'At a Police Station' is now defined as within the boundary of any building or enclosed yard that forms part of the Police Station.

Questioning about the offence
- Care needs to be taken where for example an MCQ relates to the DP being arrested in another police area.
- So long as they only question the DP about the offence in that area, the relevant time clock for an offence in another area will not begin UNLESS they question him about that offence!

Surrender to Bail
- When a DP surrenders to bail, the clock does NOT start again. The DP's previous time in custody must be noted. So if he/she was previously in custody for 15 hours then he has 9 hours left!

QUESTION

ANDERSON is arrested by Police Constable PATEL on suspicion of a shoplifting. PC PATEL conducts a search of his house under Section 18(5) of PACE, however, prior to taking him to the police station, and while leaving the house after the search, ANDERSON is taken ill. PC PATEL takes him direct to hospital where he is bailed under s.30A of PACE. ANDERSON answers his bail at the Police Station a week later.

At what point in time does the relevant time begin?

A. At the time of arrest.
B. At the time the search begins.
C. When ANDERSON arrives at Hospital.
D. When ANDERSON answers bail.

Answer D.

When he answers bail, unless, of course, ANDERSON is questioned in relation to the offence.

Detained Persons Right to Have Someone Informed of their Arrest

Where a person is

| in police detention | in connection with an | & not charged |

INDICTABLE offence

his rights to have someone notified of his arrest may be delayed

IF

⬇

an **INSPECTOR** or above has reasonable grounds for **BELIEVING** that the exercise of either right **WILL**

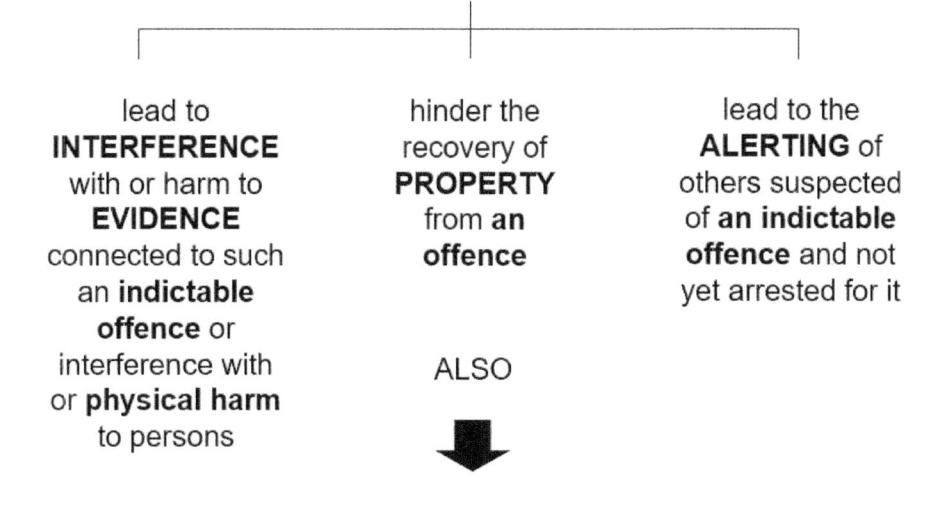

| lead to **INTERFERENCE** with or harm to **EVIDENCE** connected to such an **indictable offence** or interference with or **physical harm** to persons | hinder the recovery of **PROPERTY** from an **offence** | lead to the **ALERTING** of others suspected of **an indictable offence** and not yet arrested for it |

ALSO

⬇

```
         ┌──────────┴──────────┐
  benefit from their      the recovery of property
   criminal conduct       constituting the benefit
     (POCA 2002)              will be hindered
```

These rights may be delayed only for as long as GROUNDS EXIST

Police Detention
- Taken to a police station after arrest for an offence or under S41 TACT 2000 (provides a constable with a power to arrest anyone they reasonably suspect to be a terrorist).
- Arrested at a police station after attending voluntarily or accompanying a police officer to it & is detained there or elsewhere in the charge of a constable.
- Also applies to designated escort officers taking a detained person to a police station.

Right to have someone informed
- Applies to *one person* known to him.
- Two alternatives *may* be chosen if the first cannot be contacted.
- Anymore is at the discretion of CO.

OR
- officer in charge of the investigation.

OR
- Someone who is likely to take an interest in his welfare informed at public expense of his whereabouts as soon as practicable.

Transfers to another station
- The same right applies on arrival.
- Known as the right not to be held incommunicado.

Authorisation
- The authorisation may be made *orally* either in person or *by telephone* BUT must be *recorded in writing as soon as practicable*.

Juveniles
- An appropriate Adult MUST be informed in every case.
- It may not be the AA the juvenile wants.
- The delay actually relates to any OTHER person the detained person wishes to be informed.

Terrorism Offences
- Increases authority from Inspector to Superintendent.

PACE s.18
- There is no requirement to make this notification by the fastest method such as by telephone the phone so if a s.18 Search is to be conducted relatively quickly then the notification could take place then.
- Lengthy delay, however, may breach HRA.

Authorisation for visits
- This is determined by CO.
- Denial may be based on:
  - Hindrance to investigation;
  - Lack of 'manpower' to supervise the visit.

Maximum time limit for delay?

⬇

36 hours from the relevant time

Terrorism cases?

⬇

48 hours from the relevant time

Q. Sergeant Davies, the Custody officer, has a murder suspect in custody and the Officer in the Case, a Detective Inspector wishes to authorise a delay in notification herself. Is this permissible?
A. Yes.

Relevant Time
- Generally the time of arrival at the police station, however, there are a couple of variables attached to this assertion which we'll come to shortly.

QUESTION

Which of the following circumstances is correct with regard to delaying the right to have someone informed?

A. The offence is indictable and an officer of the rank of inspector or above *not connected* to the investigation may authorise the delay.
B. The offence is indictable and an officer of the rank of inspector or above *whether or not connected* to the investigation may authorise the delay.

Answer B. The offence is indictable and an officer of the rank of inspector or above *whether or not connected* to the investigation may authorise the delay.

Detained Persons Use of a Telephone or Writing Materials

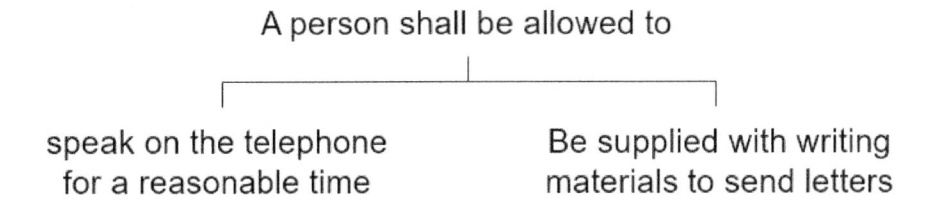

A person shall be allowed to

- speak on the telephone for a reasonable time
- Be supplied with writing materials to send letters

however in the case of

an INDICTABLE OFFENCE

This right may also be delayed by an **Inspector or above**

Note
- The circumstances under which this delay may take place are the same as for those relating to the delay in notification to have someone informed of the DP's arrest.
- Where authorisation is given the DP MUST be told that:
  - Calls will be monitored;
  - Written materials will be read;
  - Both may be used in evidence unless subject to legal privilege.

Detained Persons Right to Legal Advice

Where a person is

| in police detention | in connection with an INDICTABLE Offence | not charged |

his rights to Legal Advice may be delayed

⬇

IF

a **SUPERINTENDENT** or above has reasonable grounds for **BELIEVING** that the exercise of either right **MIGHT**

| lead to **INTERFERENCE** with or harm to **EVIDENCE** connected to such **an offence** or **interference** with or physical harm to persons | lead to the **ALERTING** of others suspected of the offence **and not yet arrested for it** | lead to **SERIOUS** loss of or damage to property | hinder the recovery of **PROPERTY** from **an offence** |

ALSO

⬇

```
                    |
        ┌───────────┴───────────┐
 benefit from their        the recovery of property
  criminal conduct          constituting the benefit
     (POCA 2002)              will be hindered
```

These rights may be delayed only for as long as GROUNDS EXIST

Note

While these rights may be delayed only for as long as GROUNDS EXIST under no circumstances can this continue beyond 36 hours from the relevant time or 48 hours in cases of Terrorism.

QUESTION

LEACH has been arrested on suspicion of driving while unfit through drink or drugs. At 11.03pm LEACH asks to consult with a solicitor. At 11.05pm the booking in procedure is complete, but is not until 11.07pm that the intoximeter room becomes available. At 11.10pm the custody officer calls the duty solicitor on behalf of LEACH who subsequently refuses to provide the requisite two evidential samples of breath.

Given these circumstances, will this seven minute delay in notifying the duty solicitor amount to a breach of s.58 PACE?

A. Yes, this delay *will* amount to a breach of s.58, but *will not* offer LEACH an excuse for refusal to provide the evidential specimens.
B. Yes, this delay *will* amount to a breach of s.58 and *will* offer LEACH a reasonable excuse for refusal to provide the evidential specimens.
C. No, this delay *will not* amount to a breach of s.58 and *will not* offer LEACH an excuse for refusal to provide the evidential specimens.
D. No, this delay *will not* amount to a breach of s.58 but *will* offer LEACH a reasonable excuse for refusal to provide the evidential specimens.

Answer A. Yes, this delay *will* amount to a breach of s.58, but *will not* offer LEACH an excuse for refusal to provide the evidential specimens.

This question relates to **Kirk v DPP (2003)** during which a seven minute delay between the request for and calling of a solicitor *was* held to be an unreasonable delay, although in this case it did not lead to the exclusion of any evidence, specifically the refusal to provide evidential breath samples.

It is also worth noting that in accordance with Campbell v DPP (2002), it is proportionate for officers to be able to go ahead with the taking of such evidential samples without the DP without legal advice having been obtained.

Solicitors
- This delay applies only to *specific* solicitors however, if the Superintendent cannot give one or more of these reasons for delaying a *specific* solicitor then this delay cannot be adopted.

Q. Other than the issues previously identified, what other reason may a superintendent have for delaying a DP's right to legal consultation?
A. Where the superintendent has RGB the solicitor requested by the DP will (not may) inadvertently or otherwise, pass on a message from the DP or act in a way which may lead to those consequences previously identified.

Note
- In this instance, the DP must be allowed to choose another solicitor.

Juveniles
- Again, an appropriate Adult MUST be informed in every case and again, may not the AA the juvenile requests.

Inferences
- If access to legal advice is denied, the drawing of adverse inferences from silence will NOT be permitted. This also means the OLD style caution would need to be used, albeit in such rare instances.

QUESTION

GREEN is held for an offence under the Terrorism Act 2000. Inspector BROWN wishes to be present while GREEN consults with his solicitor.

Given these circumstances, which of the following statements is correct?

A. The officer present must be a uniformed inspector or above, not connected with the investigation and authorised by a superintendent or above.
B. The officer present must be a uniformed inspector or above, not connected with the investigation and authorised by an Assistant Chief Constable or Commander.
C. The officer present must be an inspector or above, not connected with the investigation and authorised by a superintendent or above.
D. The officer present must be an inspector or above, not connected with the investigation and authorised by an Assistant Chief Constable or Commander.

Answer B. The officer present must be a uniformed inspector or above, not connected with the investigation and authorised by an Assistant Chief Constable or Commander.

Representations

The following shall be given the opportunity to make representations

- Detainee
- Solicitor (if available)
- Responsible adult (if available)

Any other person having an interest in the detained person's welfare MAY make representations

Representations
- May be made *orally* or in *writing*, the relevant document being retained.
- The CO can refuse to hear the representation from the DP when they are unfit.

QUESTION

ROBERTS is in Police Detention on suspicion of a Robbery. His appropriate adult believes that ROBERTS detention is unlawful and wishes to apply to a court for his release.

Is the appropriate adult permitted to make this application to the court?

A. No, only a legal representative may make the application under these circumstances.
B. No, such applications may only be made through a Superintendent.
C. Yes, however, the application may only be made by the Appropriate Adult.
D. Yes, however, the application may be made by any representative of the person.

Answer D. Yes, however, the application may be made by any representative of the person. This is called the principle of habeas corpus whereby if any person representing a DP does not feel the detention is lawful, he/she may apply to the court for the detainee's release.

Reviews of Detention

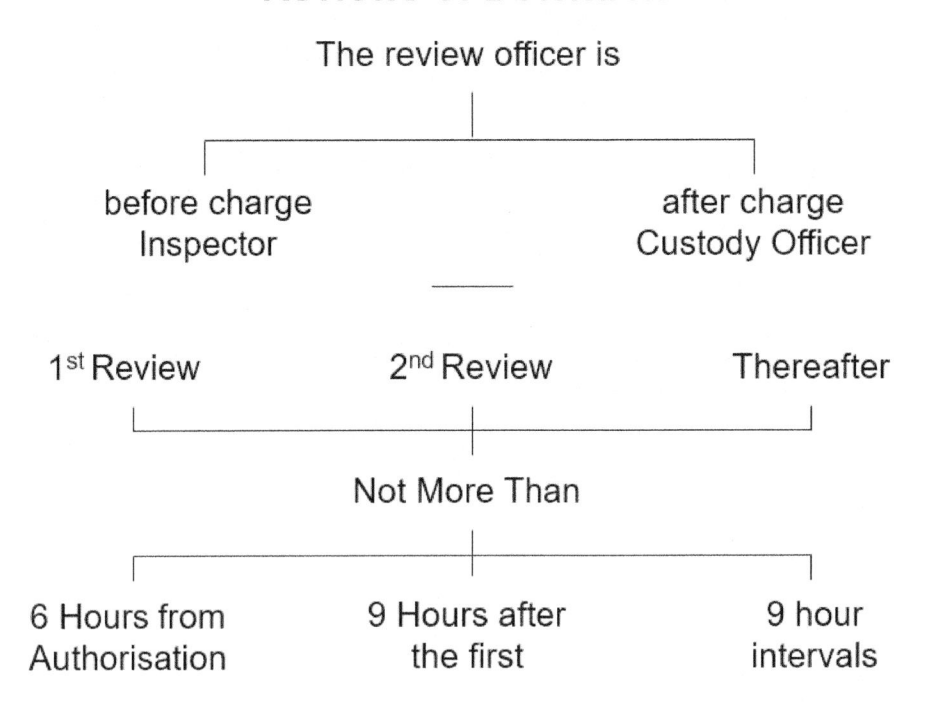

The review officer is

- before charge: Inspector
- after charge: Custody Officer

1st Review	2nd Review	Thereafter

Not More Than

6 Hours from Authorisation	9 Hours after the first	9 hour intervals

Note
- Unlike the relevant time clock which begins on arrival at the police station, the *review clock* begins from the time at which the DPs detention is authorised by the custody officer.

Before Charge
- Inspector *not* involved in the investigation.

Review times begin from the time the custody officer authorises detention
- Which means there are now 2 clocks running for the DP:
    o Relevant time;
    o Review time.

Reviews
- The 6, 9 & 9 reviews are the *maximum* times at which reviews may be left, however they may be brought forward e.g. a night duty Inspector may do all the reviews at say 2200 hrs thus allowing the detainees an uninterrupted night's sleep.
- If the review is late then the subsequent review will take place from when it should have been done and not the actual time.

Telephone Reviews
- Section 40A of PACE, allows telephone reviews *but* if live link is available and practicable to use the this *must* be used and a telephone review is not permitted.

ALSO

- Telephone reviews will *not* be conducted after charge.

QUESTION

Where a review officer considers there is sufficient evidence to charge a detained person and having authorised continued detention only for charge, which of the following applies should the custody officer disagree?

A. It is suggested the custody officer must either charge or release the detained person with or without bail.
B. Given these circumstances the matter should be referred to a superintendent or above.

Answer A.

Wake up the DP for a review?
- No, but the DP must be informed of the decision and reason ASAP on waking.

HOWEVER

- The DP MUST be awake for extensions of detention!

QUESTION

RACHELL has been arrested on suspicion of False Representation. After interview the arresting officer is discussing the case with the Custody Officer as the Review Officer arrives. The Custody Officer believes there is sufficient evidence to charge RACHELL however, the Review Office, who was listening in on the conversation disagrees.

Given these circumstances with whom does the decision to charge rest?
A. The decision rests with the Custody Officer.
B. The decision rests with the Review Officer.
C. The decision will be referred to a Chief Inspector.
D. The decision will be referred to a Superintendent.

Answer A.

Note
- This is different to where the dispute is simply between the CO and an officer of a higher rank e.g. the Detective Inspector in charge of the case in which case the matter will, at once, be referred to a Superintendent or above with responsibility for the station.
- The same also applies to a similar dispute between the Review Officer and an officer of a higher rank.

Terrorism Act 2000

Where a person has been detained under the Terrorism Act 2000

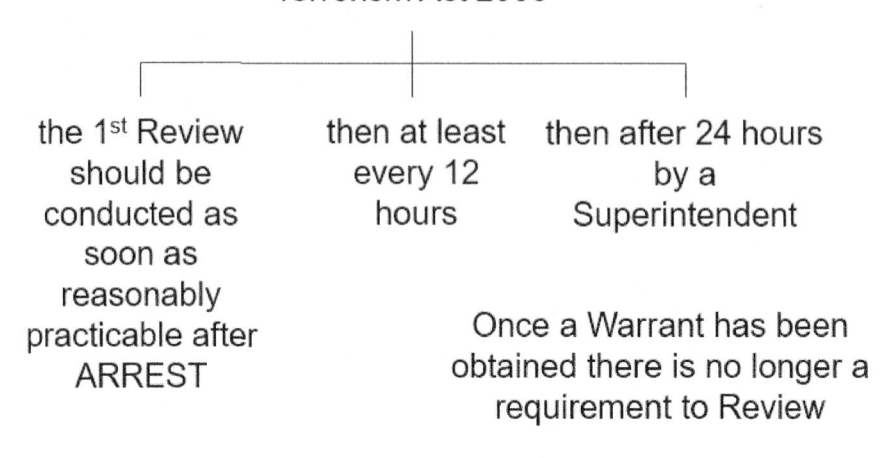

- the 1st Review should be conducted as soon as reasonably practicable after ARREST
- then at least every 12 hours
- then after 24 hours by a Superintendent

Once a Warrant has been obtained there is no longer a requirement to Review

Note
- The Relevant Time ALSO begins at time of arrest.

Review by telephone?
- NO, not in this instance.

Disclosure of Identity
- Is NO longer restricted to Terrorism cases and now applies to any officer or support staff member *if they reasonably believe that by doing so they might put themselves in danger*. (Code C para 2.6A)

Postponement of Review

A review may be postponed if

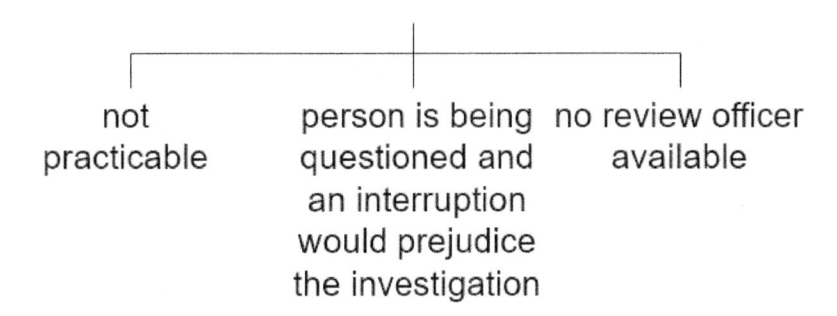

- not practicable
- person is being questioned and an interruption would prejudice the investigation
- no review officer available

Not practicable
- Detainee on an ID Parade when the review falls.

False Imprisonment
- When a review fails to be completed and is not done for a lawful reason then the detainee may sue for false imprisonment.

Postponement
- Subsequent reviews must take place not more than 9 hours after the *actual time the previous review was due* and not 9 hours after the postponed review.

QUESTION

RICHARDS has been arrested for a Breach of the Peace and is being held overnight at the local Police Station.

In accordance with PACE, is a review of his detention required?
A. Yes.
B. No.

Answer B.

Note
- Not according to PACE, however, in this case, best practice indicates the need to regularly review a DP's detention even though Breach of the Peace is not an 'offence'.
- This type of review can be conducted by a CO.
- The same applies to other circumstances such the execution of an arrest warrant for 'Fail to Appear' as the DP is being held in custody on behalf of the prison service.
- Where bail has been refused this decision to refuse bail must be reviewed by the Custody Officer (in the same manner required by a Review Officer) every 9 hours until the person is taken to court.

Bail

Where bail has been **refused** this decision must be **reviewed by the Custody Officer** (in the same manner required by a Review Officer) **every 9 hours** until the person is taken to court

⬇

The **Custody Officer may detain a person after charge** for **up to 6 hours** if he/she has reasonable grounds for **BELIEVING** the detention of the person is necessary to enable a sample to be taken under s. 63B PACE

UNLESS

That extends beyond 24 hours (Relevant Time)

Testing for Class 'A' Substances

Where a person is in police detention a

- sample of urine **or** non Intimate Sample

may be taken
(NOT BY FORCE)

to ascertain whether he/she has any specified Class 'A' drug in their body

Conditions

Over 18 charged or arrested with

Theft	OR	an OFFENCE & an officer of at least the rank of Inspector has RGS the misuse caused or contributed to the offence
Robbery		
Burglary (incl Agg)		
TWC (incl Agg)		
Handling		
Fraud		
Going Equipped		
Supply, possession or possession with intent to supply class 'A' drug etc.		**14 or over but Under 18, applies only when charged**

Note -

- The Custody Officer may detain a person after charge for *up to 6 hours* if he/she has reasonable grounds for *believing* the detention of the person is necessary to enable a sample to be taken under s. 63B PACE

UNLESS

- That extends beyond 24 hours (Relevant Time).

Authorisation
- May be given orally or in writing, but when oral this must be confirmed in writing asap.

Rights
- Before taking the sample the person must be reminded of their rights, warned that a failure to provide is an offence & be told of the reason for the requirement.

Reasons
- Decide whether to grant Bail or not.
- Re supervision when already remand.
- Sentencing.
- Appropriate Advice & Treatment.

The 3 Search Levels

In order to safeguard the detained person there are 3 levels to which a search may be conducted

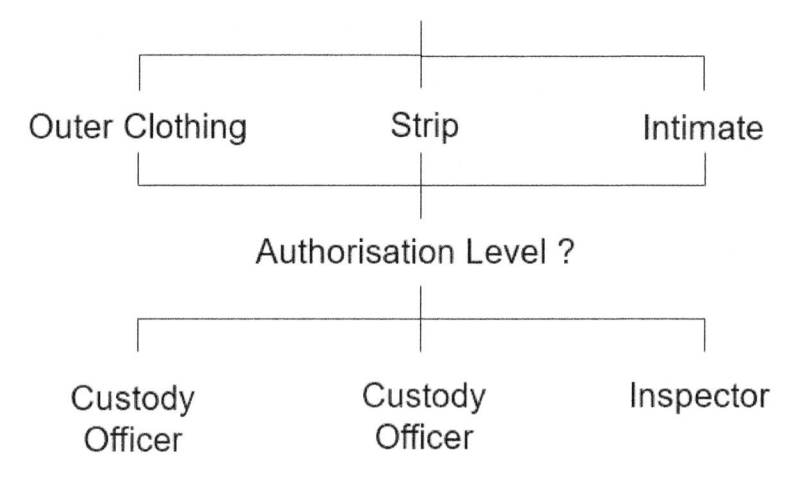

```
                    |
      ┌─────────────┼─────────────┐
Outer Clothing     Strip        Intimate
      └─────────────┼─────────────┘
                    |
            Authorisation Level ?
                    |
      ┌─────────────┼─────────────┐
   Custody       Custody       Inspector
   Officer       Officer
```

Do searches have to be conducted?
- No, if the DP is not going to be placed in a cell or in detention for a short time (custody records should be endorsed 'not searched')

HOWEVER
- If the detainee refuses to sign the custody record, the CO will be obliged to ascertain what property they have on them.
- The extent of the search is determined by CO's *honestly held belief* that it is necessary.

Outer Clothing
- Also includes shoes, sock, removal of jewellery, pat downs etc.

Strip
- Removal of more than outer clothing, including examining a persons mouth.
- Does not automatically mean a search of the whole person.
- Indications from a metal detector *may* give grounds for the CO to authorise a strip search.

Who present?
- Exposure of intimates parts - *at least* 2 persons of the same sex.
- Juvenile - 1 of the 2 *must* be an Appropriate Adult (AA).

UNLESS
- The juvenile signifies otherwise IN THE PRESENCE of the AA.

Property
- Must be returned to the DP on release unless seized & retained for evidential purposes.

Q. Under what circumstances may a Custody Officer seize clothing and personal effects from a detained person?
A. The Custody Officer believes the detained person *may* use them to cause...
H arm (physical injury) to self or others
E scape or assist him to escape
E vidence (interference with)
D amage to property

Q. Under what circumstances shall more than 2 persons (other than the Appropriate Adult) be permitted to conduct the search?
A. Exceptional Circumstances.

Q. Where a strip search involves the exposure of intimate parts, under what circumstances will it be necessary to have less than 2 people present OR in the case of a juvenile, the Appropriate Adult?
A. Urgent cases where there is a risk of SERIOUS harm to the detainee or others.

Q. When the detained person is required to bend over for a visual examination of the genital area, what happens if an item is seen protruding from the anus?
A. The detained person will be asked to hand it over. Refusal = Intimate Search

Intimate Searches

Where an **INSPECTOR** or above has reasonable cause for **BELIEVING** that an arrested person may have concealed anything which

- he might use to cause physical injury to themselves or another at the station
- is a Class A drug which they intended to supply or export

a search may be authorised

Intimate Search
- Means a search of body orifices other than the mouth.
- Inspector must be satisfied that an intimate search is the only practical means of removing an item.
- The search may *only* be carried out by a registered medical practitioner or registered nurse.

UNLESS
- Inspector or above *considers* this is not practicable and *sufficiently severe*, then a police officer *may* carry out the search.
- Requires written consent from the DP and in the case of a *drug* search *should* be conducted by registered medical practitioner or registered nurse.
- Refusal requires the DP to be informed of the consequences namely that refusal with out good cause may harm his/her defence should the case go to Trial.

Where the search may take place?
- Drug offence Not at a police station.
- Otherwise Police station, hospital, doctor's surgery, a place used for medical purposes.

Drug search - how many persons present?
- Minimum 2.

Same Sex
- A constable may not carry out an intimate search of a person of the opposite sex.

Juveniles / Vulnerable Persons
- Unlike the strip search, the AA must be of the same sex unless the subject specifically requests for an AA of the opposite sex to be present *subject to being readily available*.

Records
- The custody officer must record which parts of the body were searched, who carried out the search, who was present, the reasons for the search and the results.

Embarrassment
- Every effort must be made to reduce to the minimum the embarrassment that a person may experience.

X Rays and Ultrasound

Soundbites

INSPECTOR or above has reasonable grounds for **BELIEVING** that an arrested person has

- **Swallowed a Class A Drug**

  and was in possession with intent to supply to another or export

- **Conducted by a RMP or RN at Hospital, Surgery or other medical establishment**

  Written consent required plus warning re refusal

GENERAL PRINCIPLES
POLICE POWERS & PROCEDURES

SESSION 3

IDENTIFICATION

When an Identification Procedure MUST be Held

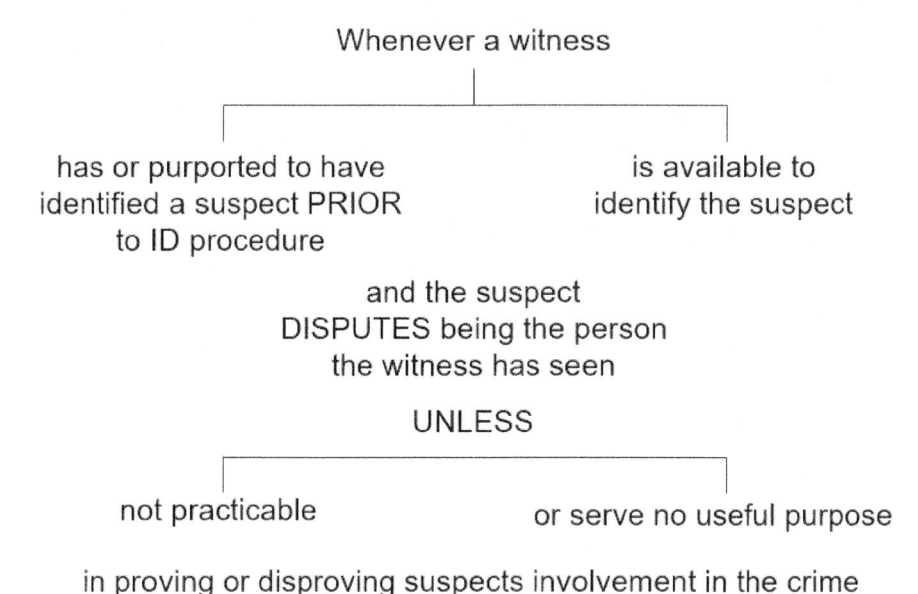

Whenever a witness

has or purported to have identified a suspect PRIOR to ID procedure

is available to identify the suspect

and the suspect DISPUTES being the person the witness has seen

UNLESS

not practicable

or serve no useful purpose

in proving or disproving suspects involvement in the crime

PRIOR to ID Procedure
- Does *not* apply to Photo ID procedure.

Available to identify suspect
- Also requires the witness to *express an ability to identify the suspect* OR *where there is a reasonable chance they may be able to do so*, so watch out for the ONLY options AND again subject to them not already having engaged in a Video, ID Parade or Group ID procedure.

Disputes
- Also applies where such a dispute *might reasonably be anticipated*.

Not practicable
- No reasonable possibility that witness would be able to make an identification.

R v Jamel (1993)
- Access to mixed race volunteers was impracticable as it would have taken too long to arrange, therefore Group ID used instead (just because the suspect has an unusual physical feature, this does NOT necessarily preclude the provision of an ID procedure e.g. could conceal the feature OR replicate the feature on the volunteers).

R v Britton & Richards (1989)
- All reasonable steps *must* be taken to investigate the possibility of one identification option before moving onto the alternative *including* an offer from the defence solicitor to find volunteers.

Serve no useful purpose
- Suspect well known to witness who claims to have seen them commit the crime – this is different to the suspect being well known to the witness who claims to have seen them at the scene of the crime e.g. R v Chen (2001) where the defendants confirmed their presence at the scene BUT NOT their involvement in the crime SO the ID procedure did NOT apply.

ALSO

D v DPP (1998) and R v Haynes (2004)
- Makes it clear that where the identification is based on just clothing or age then this is NOT an identification from which an ID procedure would prove useful.

When an Identification Procedure MUST be Held cont…

MAY

also be held if

OIC

considers it would prove useful

KEY FACTOR

'Whether a failure to hold a parade could be a matter of genuine potential prejudice to the suspect'

Note
- Where it has been decided that an ID procedure is to be held, the ID officer (Inspector or above not involved in the investigation) *must* consult with each other to determine which procedure is to be offered and NOT to determine whether an ID procedure should take place.
- Once decided, it should take place ASAP.

ALSO

- The *key factor* to consider is *whether a failure to hold a parade could be a matter of genuine potential prejudice to the suspect*.

R v Graham (1994)
- Also, a suspect's failure to request an ID Parade does not mean the police may proceed without one.

Control of the Identification Process

The arrangements for and conduct of identification procedures is the responsibility of an officer

⬇

not below the rank of Inspector

however

the identification officer may allow another officer or police staff approved person to make arrangements for and to conduct the procedure.

Note
- Where it is proposed to hold an ID process at a later date certain criteria must be explained to the suspect. This can be done by the *custody officer* or *any officer not involved in the investigation* before the suspect leaves the station.
- When dealing with a witness *who is or appears* to be mentally disordered, mentally vulnerable person or a juvenile, the process *should* take place in the presence of a *Pre-Trial Support person* (no prompting and also not a witness).
- This process may be *delayed* until after arrangements for images to be taken of the suspect for use in video identification BUT only if the *OIC and IO have RGS* that given the information, the suspect would take steps to avoid identification.
- If the ID officer allows an approved person to arrange and conduct the procedure then he/she must be able to:
    - Supervise effectively and EITHER (NOT BOTH)
    - Intervene or
    - Be available to be contacted for advice.

Identification by Witnesses

Generally, identification by witnesses can be divided into occasions when the identity of the suspect is

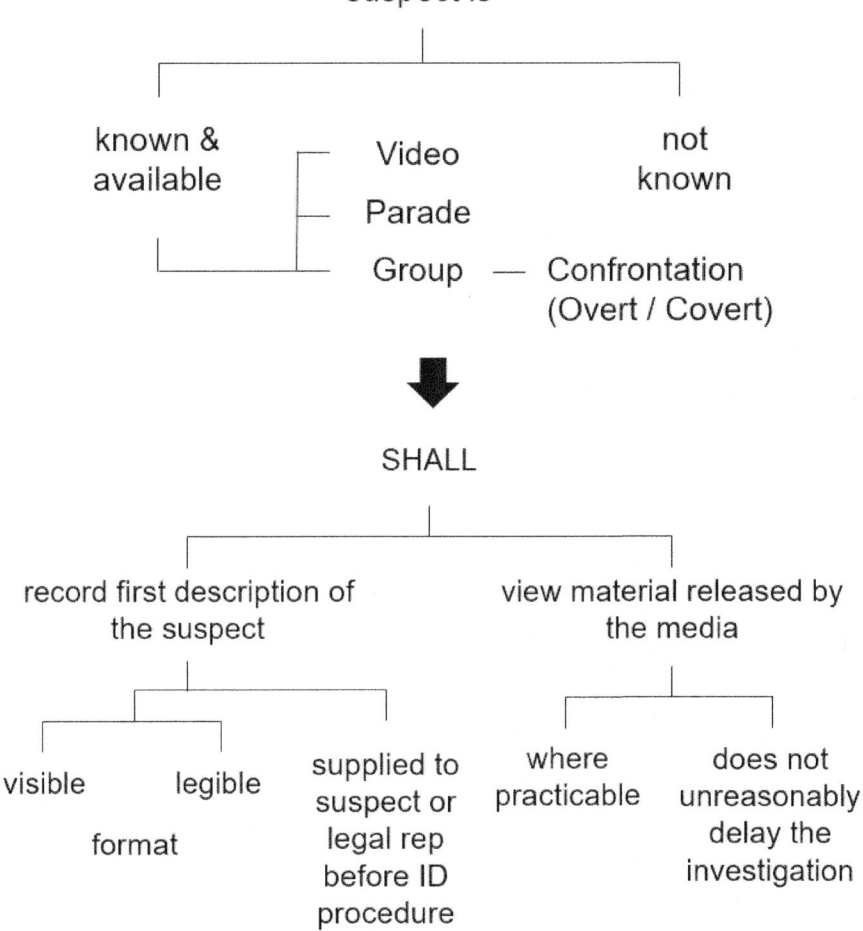

- known & available
  - Video
  - Parade
  - Group — Confrontation (Overt / Covert)
- not known

⬇

SHALL

- record first description of the suspect
  - visible
  - legible
  - format
  - supplied to suspect or legal rep before ID procedure
- view material released by the media
  - where practicable
  - does not unreasonably delay the investigation

Known
- Means there is sufficient information known of a person to justify arrest for suspected involvement in the case.
- Once a person becomes a known suspect, any witnesses, *including police officers,* who might be used at an ID Parade, are kept apart from the suspect, as any contact could jeopardise a conviction.

R v Lennon (1999)
- Arrested on description after a public order incident where the witnesses to the event, the officers, accidentally went in the van and identified the suspect. This identification was excluded.

Available
- Means the suspect is immediately available OR will be available in a reasonably short period of time and is willing to take an effective part in at least one of the following:
- Video Identification (Ratio 1: at least 8 or 2: at least 12);
- Identification Parade (Ratio 1: at least 8 or 2: at least 12);
- Group Identification.

Confrontation
- Remains a last resort & does not require the consent of the suspect.
- Suggested as a possible option where the subject is known and *unavailable* i.e. not willing to take part in the process.

Video or Parade
- These are the preferred methods and the *OIC* in consultation with the *Identification* Officer as to which option to choose and offer to the suspect.
- Suspect/AA or Solicitor may make representations.

Group ID
- May be offered:
    - If the *OIC* considers it would be more suitable than video or ID Parade *and* Identification Officer, who is responsible for setting it up considers it practical to arrange;
    - Can be moving or static e.g. coming off an escalator, in a shopping centre restaurant area.

QUESTION

What if a group ID is not practicable or suspect refuses to cooperate?

A. The officer in the case has the discretion to make arrangements for a covert video or group id to take place.
B. The identification officer has the discretion to make arrangements for a covert video or group id to take place.

Answer B.

QUESTION

Can force be used for any of these procedures?

A. Yes.
B. No.

Answer B.

Not Known
- Witness may be taken to a particular place where they saw the person on a previous occasion where the principles of a Group ID will be observed

OR
- Identification by Street ID.

QUESTION

Having attended the scene of a suspected dwelling burglary in progress Police Constable BOWES sees a suspect emptying drawers in the living room. The suspect spots him and makes off via a rear door to the premises. PC BOWES circulates his description. A short while later a male who fits the suspects description, but denies being involved in the burglary is stopped and arrested nearby. Concerned re breaching PACE, PC BOWES contacts PS HAQUE to see if he can attend the scene to identify the detained person.

Which of the following is the correct advice provided by PS HAQUE to PC BOWES?

A. Attend the scene to determine the suspect's involvement via a street identification procedure.
B. Record in writing the suspect's description prior to attending the scene for street identification.
C. Return to the station to verify suspect's identify on arrival at the custody centre.
D. Avoid contact with the suspect until invited to take part in an alternative identification procedure.

Answer D.
This case relates to R v Nunes (2001) where the officer did attend the scene and identified the suspect. This identification was subsequently deemed a breach of PACE by the Court of Appeal on the basis that having already been arrested prior to the arrival of the officer and also having denied being involved in the offence, this amounted to 'Disputed Identification Evidence' and as such the officer should have kept himself to himself with a view to providing a formal identification via an alternative ID procedure.

ALSO

It's worth noting that the requirement for the recording of a description does not necessarily have to be in writing e.g. PNB i.e. could be a quicker method such as on tape and bearing in mind all radio interactions are stored electronically this would apply.

Consent to Identification Procedures

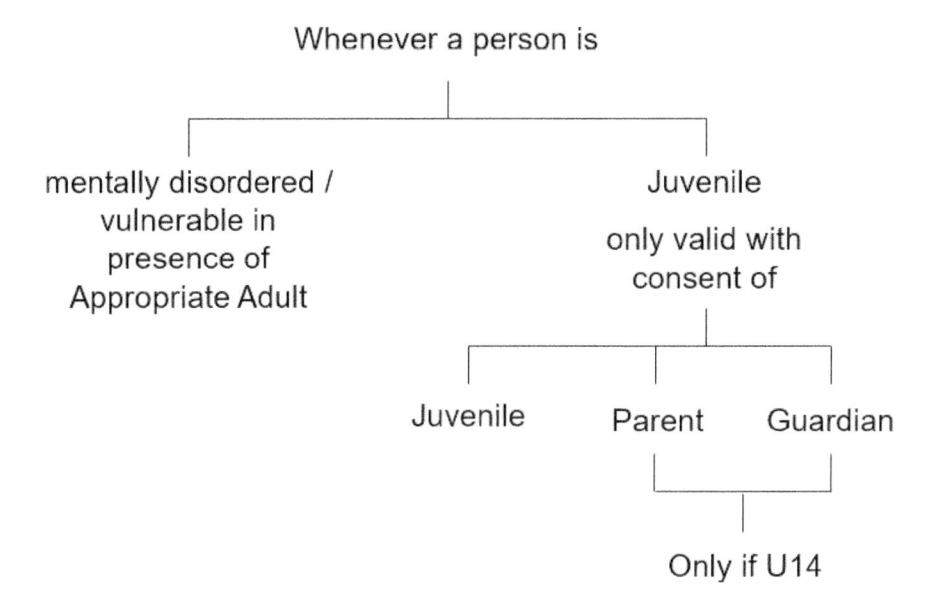

Whenever a person is

- mentally disordered / vulnerable in presence of Appropriate Adult
- Juvenile — only valid with consent of
  - Juvenile
  - Parent
  - Guardian

Only if U14 (Parent / Guardian)

Appropriate Adult
- If an AA is not present when the procedural information is provided, then it must be repeated when he/she arrives.

Witnesses
- For those persons who appear to be mentally disordered / vulnerable or juveniles, again, a pre-trial support person will be present during the procedure unless the witness states they do not want a support person present.

Checking Documentation

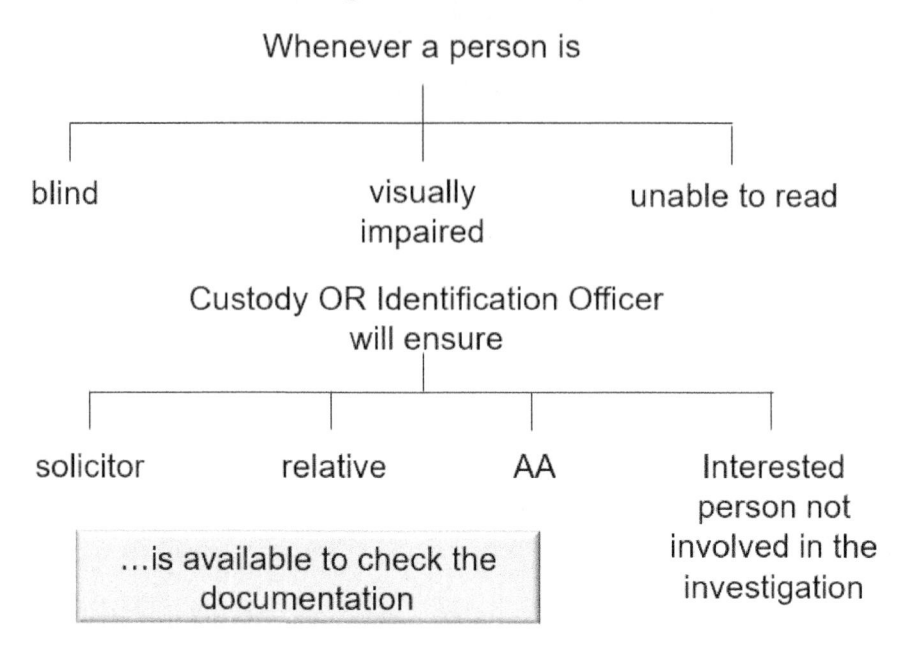

Whenever a person is
- blind
- visually impaired
- unable to read

Custody OR Identification Officer will ensure
- solicitor
- relative
- AA
- Interested person not involved in the investigation

...is available to check the documentation

Q. Who is responsible for signing the documentation?
A. The person *or representative at the person's consent.*

Q. What if the person refuses to sign?
A. The representative by seeking to protect the interests of BOTH the police and suspect.

Identification of Police Officers / Staff

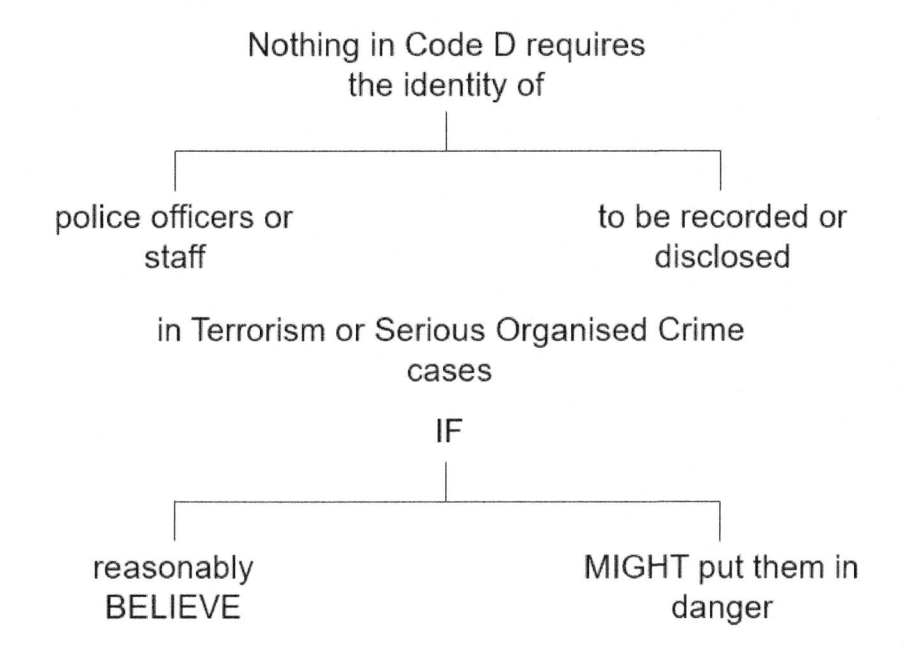

Nothing in Code D requires the identity of

- police officers or staff
- to be recorded or disclosed

in Terrorism or Serious Organised Crime cases

IF

- reasonably BELIEVE
- MIGHT put them in danger

QUESTION

If in doubt as to whether the identification of an officer should be given, which of the following is correct?

A. Consult with the custody officer or above.
B. Consult with an inspector or above.
C. Consult with the PACE inspector.
D. Consult a superintendent or above.

Answer B.

Video Identification

Eye witness to be shown MOVING images of a known suspect UNLESS

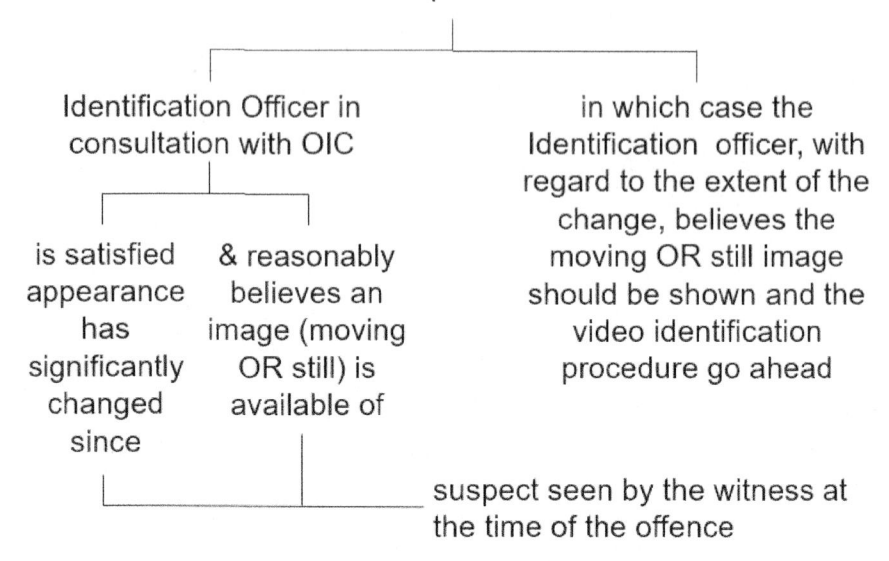

- **Identification Officer in consultation with OIC**
  - is satisfied appearance has significantly changed since
  - & reasonably believes an image (moving OR still) is available of

  _____ suspect seen by the witness at the time of the offence

- **in which case the Identification officer, with regard to the extent of the change, believes the moving OR still image should be shown and the video identification procedure go ahead**

Appearance has significantly changed
- Applies to aging or other physical changes or differences.
- In such instances, the suspect *must* be given the opportunity to provide their own images for use in the procedure BUT it's for the IO in consultation with the OIC to decide whether the image(s) can be used.

QUESTION

How many times will the eye witness be shown video images before being required to make a decision?

A. 1.
B. 2.
C. 3.
D. 4.

Answer B.

QUESTION

How many additional images to that of one suspect are shown for video identification purposes?

A. 6.
B. 8.
C. 10.
D. 12.

Answer B.

QUESTION

How many additional images to that of two suspect are shown for video identification purposes?

A. 6.
B. 8.
C. 10.
D. 12.

Answer D.

Identification Parades

The ratio of suspect(s) to persons involved in an Identification Parade is

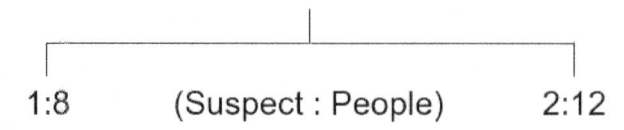

- 1:8
- (Suspect : People)
- 2:12

Required to resemble the suspect(s) as far as possible in

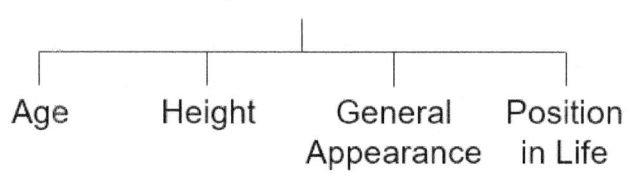

- Age
- Height
- General Appearance
- Position in Life

Q. What happens where unusual features such as scars and tattoos cannot be replicated?
A. The feature may be concealed.

Q. Can police officers in uniform stand on an ID Parade?
A. Yes, subject to numbers / badges being concealed.

QUESTION

Can the suspect choose where to stand on an ID Parade?

A. Yes.
B. No.

Answer A.

QUESTION

How many eye witnesses may be shown an ID Parade at any one time?

A. 1
B. 2.
C. 3.
D. 4.

Answer A.

QUESTION

How many times must the eye witness look at each person before making a decision?

A. Once.
B. At least twice.
C. At least three.
D. At least four.

Answer B.

QUESTION

What happens if an eye witness makes an identification after the ID Parade has finished?

A. Inform the suspect, solicitor Interpreter or friend.
B. Inform the suspect, solicitor Interpreter or friend then conduct a second Parade.
C. Conduct a second ID Parade without informing the suspect, solicitor, interpreter or friend.
D. Inform the suspect, solicitor Interpreter or friend then consider conducting a second Parade.

Answer D.

Q. What happens once the ID Parade has concluded?
A. The suspect will be asked if they want to comment.

QUESTION

On his way home from the pub, ELLIS is set upon and robbed by a group of men. One of the suspects, SCANES, is subsequently arrested and agrees to take part in an Identification Parade. Despite being told to only pick out one person, ELLIS identifies SCANES along with another person on the Parade. All other aspects of the identification procedure were conducted correctly.

In accordance with PACE Code D, Annex B which of the following statements is correct in terms of the probative (proof) value of this identification?

A. Where more than one identification is made, the potential probative value of the identification will not be negatively affected.
B. Where any such breach is made, the probative value of the identification will be negatively affected.
C. So long as both persons looked alike, the potential probative value of the identification will not be negatively affected.
D. Despite both persons looking alike, the potential probative value of the identification will be negatively affected.

Answer C.

The key here is that all other aspects of the identification procedure were conducted correctly and as such given the judgement on Appeal in the case of Abdullah, Pululu v R (2019) the identification evidence was correctly admitted as potentially probative.

Needless to say however, any such failures to follow the Codes will see the defence seeking to have the identification evidence excluded, some instances of which are blindingly obvious as, to coin a turn of phrase, being 'bang out of order,' such as in R v Jones (1999) in which the suspect was told force would be used against him if he didn't comply with the parade.

The showing of photos ahead of the procedure or the OIC getting involved, also falls into this category while genuine mistakes will be judged on their individual merits and whether the identification is made less reliable.

RECOGNITION OR IDENTIFICATION

When considering the issue of **RECOGNITION OR IDENTIFICATION** this is where a witness states they **know the offender as opposed to providing a description**.

In which of the following instances will an identification procedure be required?

Q. Witness identified masked attacker from his voice and eyes?

A. R v DAVIES (2004) A witness identified a masked attacker from his voice and eyes i.e. recognised him. The court held that this ID, coupled with other circumstantial evidence, was sufficient for a conviction, so Recognition not Identification watch out for the ONLY, MAY or WILL question options.

Q. Witness discovered name of suspect from a third party?

A. R v C; R v B (2003) A witness did not initially know the name of the suspect, but later found out from a third party i.e. the victim still recognised the person, just didn't know his name until such time as his school chums gave him the information so again Recognition not Identification.

Q. Suspect denies they are well known to the witness?

A. H v DPP (2003) The court held that where a defendant accepted they were well known to a witness, it was not necessary to hold a parade. This was a matter of recognition not of identification and therefore ID procedure not necessary.

HOWEVER

R v Harris (2002) Where the question of recognition was *disputed* by the defendant, in this case via a prepared statement an ID procedure should have taken place.

Q. What if the suspect is recognised having seen CCTV / film / photographic footage?

A. Recognition.

Q. Will partial views of a suspect be sufficient for the purposes of recognition?

A. R v Lariba (2015) Two local off duty police officers recognised a gang member suspected of murder, even though they were not in a position to make notes, but were able to recognise him from a variety of factors including demeanour, skin tone, hairline, eyebrows and clothing. These factors along with their familiarity with the suspect contributed to a reliable identification by means of recognition.

Q. What about recognising a person via Facebook?

A. R v McCullough (2011) In this instance, a formal identification was required, so not recognition.

Q. Can facial mapping be used for evidential purposes of recognition?

A. R v Purlis (2017) Required an expert in facial mapping to piece together evidence from a dashboard camera capturing images of a suspect making off from the scene of a robbery HOWEVER the wording in this case talked of lending 'powerful support to the contention that the images were of the same man.'

Photo IDs

Sergeant or above to

supervise & direct

Showing may be done by a

constable or civilian police employee

- First Description
- One witness at a time
- 12 Photos at a time
- Positive ID
- Separate Photo

Note
- Used where the suspect is NOT known.

First description
- Must be recorded *before* the witness sees the photos.

12 Photos
- Must be roughly the same and shown at the same time i.e. not one after the other and be told the suspects photo may or may not be there.

Positive ID
- Once made no other witnesses will be shown the photos, remaining witnesses being invited onto an ID Parade, unless no dispute re the identification.

Separate photo
- To be taken of the frame in order that it may be reconstructed, the original photos being retained for production in court if necessary.

R v Lamb (1980) and **R v Allen (1996)**
- Using photos from police records can affect the judgement of the jury and nothing should be done to draw their attention to this fact UNLESS the jury are already aware of the defendant's previous convictions.

Destruction and Retention of Suspect Photographs Taken or USED in Eyewitness Procedures

Photos MUST be destroyed
UNLESS Suspect

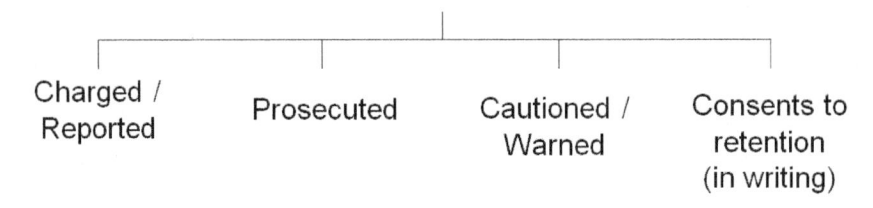

| Charged / Reported | Prosecuted | Cautioned / Warned | Consents to retention (in writing) |

Photos may ONLY be taken for purposes related to

| **Prevention / Detection of Crime** | **Investigation of Offences** | **Conduct of Prosecutions** |

Fingerprints / Non- Intimate Samples with Consent

'Appropriate Consent'

For the purposes of taking fingerprints, the meaning of appropriate consent is in relation to

Under 14
Parent or Guardian

-

14, 15 or 16
Parent or Guardian and CHILD

-

17
That person

Note
- Consent *must* be in *writing*.
- Definition of fingerprints include Palm prints and *may be recorded by any means not just a print*.
- Skin impressions, in relation to any person, means any record (other than a fingerprint) which is a record in any form and produced by any method) of the skin pattern and other physical characteristics or features of the whole or any part of his foot or of any other part of his body.

Non-Intimate Samples

Sample of hair (not pubic), which includes plucked from the root

-

Sample taken from nail or under nail

-

A swab taken from any part of the body (including mouth) other than a part from which would be an intimate sample

-

Saliva

-

Skin impression from the body, other than a fingerprint

Note
- Sample of hair should be plucked individually so not a handful *unless the suspect prefers otherwise* & no more than the person taking considers reasonable for a sufficient sample.

ALSO

- Suspect may also be offered a reasonable choice from where the sample is plucked.

Fingerprints
BEFORE Conviction

Fingerprints of a person detained at a police station may be taken WITHOUT consent if

- in consequence of arrest or released on bail
- has been charged or reported

for a RECORDABLE offence

- and has not had fingerprints taken in the course of that investigation
- or fingerprints did not constitute a complete or partial set of prints suitable for analysis / comparison / matching

Non-Intimate Samples
BEFORE Conviction

A non-intimate sample may be taken from a person WITHOUT consent if

- in consequence of arrest or released on bail
- or has been charged or reported, whether or not in custody

for a RECORDABLE offence

- and has not had a non-intimate sample of the same type from same part of the body taken in the course of that investigation
- or the non-intimate sample was proved insufficient
  or
  if released on bail also not suitable

Detained
- Also applies to a person NOT detained at a police station where they have been charged or reported for an offence.

Recordable Offence
- These are offences for which convictions, cautions, reprimands or warnings are recorded in national Police Records and generally those punishable by imprisonment.

Force?
- Yes reasonable.

Age
- Applies to anyone over 10 years of age.

Released or released on bail
- The exception to the rule for taking another set of fingerprints / non-intimate sample from a person released or released on bail is where the investigation was *discontinued* then subsequently resumed, during which the sample was destroyed.

Inspectors / Court authority
- When a person answers bail at a police station or at Court, fingerprints may be taken if an *Inspector or above or the Court* so authorises orally then in writing asap where there are RGB (not RGS) the person answering bail is not the same person OR claims not to have been the person from whom the original prints were taken OR the Court so authorises.

Terrorism Act Non-Intimate Samples
- Requires superintendent authority.

Fingerprints / Non- Intimate Samples AFTER Conviction or Caution

Where a person has been

    convicted   cautioned

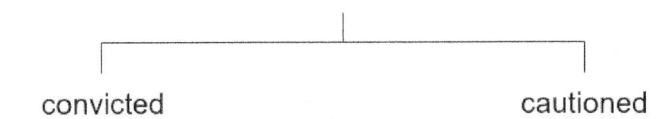

for a RECORDABLE offence and the fingerprints / non-intimate sample were either not taken, F/Ps did not constitute a complete or partial set of prints suitable for analysis / comparison / matching or the sample was insufficient or not suitable

Inspector or above

is satisfied that taking the fingerprints / non-intimate sample is necessary to

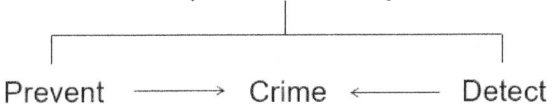

Prevent ⟶ Crime ⟵ Detect

Note

- Where a person has been convicted of an offence prior to the introduction of DNA profiling, it WILL be lawful for that person to be required to provide a non-intimate sample subject (as above) to an inspector or above being satisfied it is necessary to prevent or detect crime.

Fingerprints / Non-Intimate Samples AFTER Conviction Outside England & Wales

Applies to

| Qualifying Offences in England & Wales | fingerprints / non-intimate sample were either not taken, F/Ps did not constitute a complete or partial set of prints suitable for analysis / comparison / matching or the sample was insufficient or not suitable |

Inspector or above
is satisfied that taking the fingerprints / non-intimate sample is necessary to

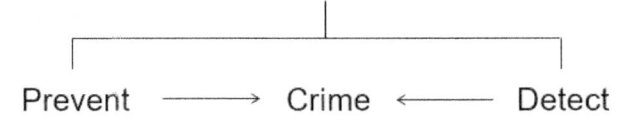

Prevent ⟶ Crime ⟵ Detect

Qualifying
- These offences are INDICTABLE offences and include:
    - Use or threat of violence;
    - Unlawful force against persons;
    - Sexual offences;
    - Offences against children.

Timeframes to Attend a Police Station to have Fingerprints / Non- Intimate Samples taken

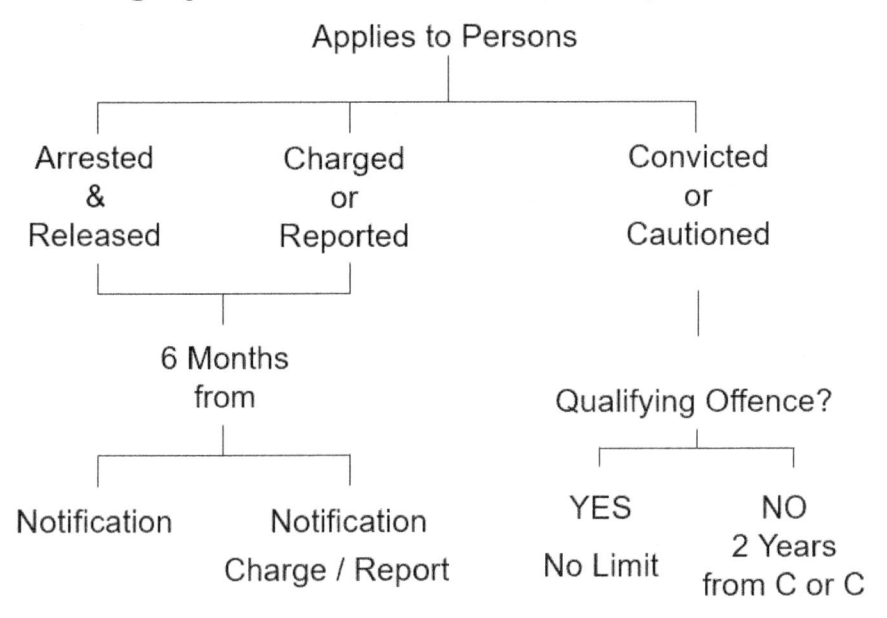

```
                        Applies to Persons
                               |
        ┌──────────────────────┼──────────────────────┐
    Arrested               Charged                Convicted
       &                     or                      or
    Released              Reported                Cautioned
        └──────────┬──────────┘                      |
                   |
              6 Months
                from                         Qualifying Offence?
           ┌───────┴───────┐                    ┌────────┴────────┐
      Notification    Notification             YES              NO
                     Charge / Report         No Limit         2 Years
                                                             from C or C
```

Note

- Notification goes to the *investigating officer* that fingerprints were incomplete or below standard OR in the event the fingerprints were destroyed prior to the resumption on the investigation, no more than 6 months from the day on which the investigation resumed.
- The person must be given *at least 7 days* notice within which to attend the police station;
- May be directed to attend at a specific time of day or between specified times;
- Officer to consider whether this could coincide with the person attending the station for another reason e.g. to sign on;
- This 7 day period need not fall within the identified period for attendance;
- May be varied by the officer if necessary in consultation with the person to whom the requirement relates;
- Inspector or above *may* authorise a period shorter than 7 days if URGENT with the facts to be recorded asap;

- If fingerprints have already been taken on 2 occasions, then further attempts must be authorised by an *Inspector or above*.
- In the event of failure to attend a constable *may arrest* without warrant.

Non-Intimate Sample
'Inspector or Above'

Where a person is held in custody under authority of the Court

Inspector or above
(in writing or oral / confirmed in writing asap)

may authorise a non-intimate sample to be taken where

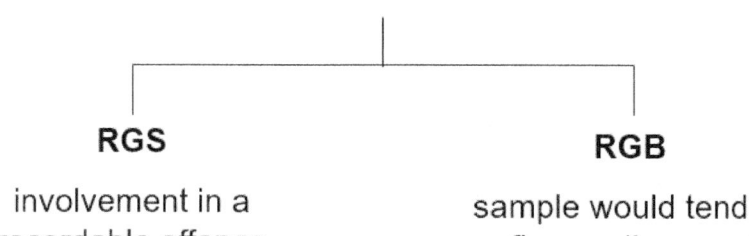

RGS
involvement in a recordable offence

RGB
sample would tend to confirm or disprove that involvement

Note
- If the first sample was taken by means of a skin impression then the second must not be taken from the same part of the body UNLESS the previous sample proved insufficient.

QUESTION

When considering the admissibility of fingerprint evidence, how many years experience must an expert witness have in this field?

A. 3.
B. 5.
C. 7.

D. 10.

Answer A. Expert fingerprint evidence the person must have at least **3 years** experience in this field (used to be 5 so watch out for this).

R v Buckley (1999)
- Highlights that expert evidence is NOT conclusive and that guilt has to be proven in light of all evidence)

QUESTION

When determining the admissibility of fingerprint evidence, how many matching ridge characteristics would be likely to qualify for inclusion as evidence in Court?

A. 8 or more.
B. 10 or more.
C. 12 or more.
D. 15 or more.

Answer A.

In determining the admissibility of fingerprint evident in court, other examples include:
- Dissimilar characteristics;
- Size of print;
- Quality & clarity.

Mobile Fingerprint Devices
'S.61 (6A) PACE'

Fingerprints using a mobile device can be taken where a constable has RGS a person

- committing
- attempting to commit
- has committed
- attempted to commit

ANY offence but not arrested IF

- name is unknown or cannot be ascertained
- reasonable grounds to DOUBT name given is real

Note
- Any offence, so recordable or otherwise.
- Fingerprints taken under this power *cannot* be checked once checked against the national fingerprint database.
- The result *may* make an arrest unnecessary on the basis that the name *has* been ascertained and therefore disposable by other means such as report, charge by post, FPN or verbal warning.

Identification of Disqualified Drivers

S.73 PACE requires PROOF that the person named on the disqualification certificate is the driver and can be obtained by means of

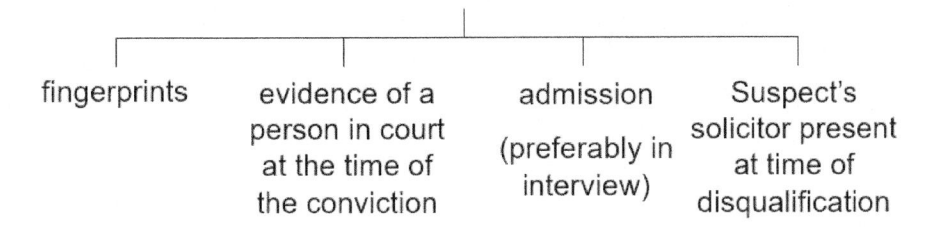

- fingerprints
- evidence of a person in court at the time of the conviction
- admission (preferably in interview)
- Suspect's solicitor present at time of disqualification

Note
- A *person in court* so not necessarily an officer.
- Admission *preferably* in interview, so not compulsory.
- Solicitor is a last resort where no other means possible.
- This is a list compiled by the court so *not exclusive*.

Speculative Search WITHOUT Consent

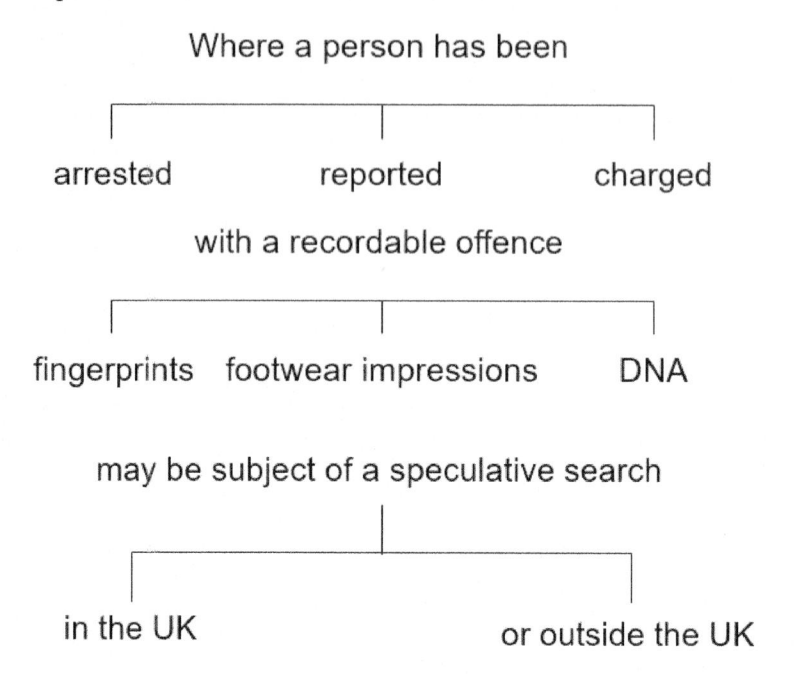

Where a person has been

- arrested
- reported
- charged

with a recordable offence

- fingerprints
- footwear impressions
- DNA

may be subject of a speculative search

- in the UK
- or outside the UK

Note
- **With consent** applies where the person is suspected of committing a recordable offence BUT is *not arrested*.

Footwear Impressions

A constable may take a persons footwear impression WITHOUT consent where they are detained at a police station

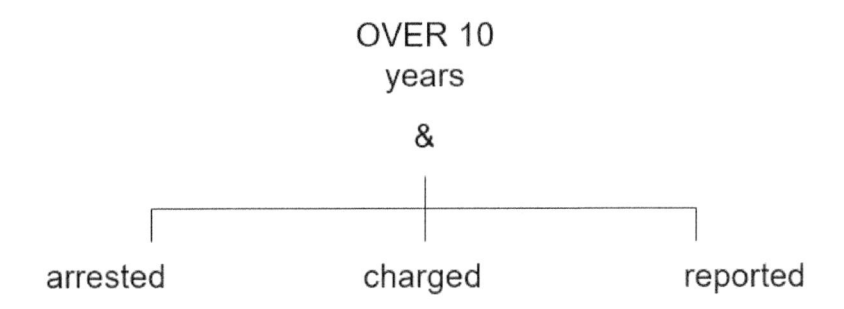

OVER 10 years

&

| arrested | charged | reported |

for a RECORDABLE offence

Note
- Reasonable Force may be used.

HOWEVER

- Requires consent UNLESS the impression has not previously been taken in the course of the investigation OR the previously taken impression is not complete / sufficient quality / comparison for matching.

R v Kempster (2008)
- An ear print be used for comparison purposes subject to where the minutiae of the ear structure can be identified and matched HOWEVER although the conviction in this case was unsuccessful, the principle of using such an impression was capable of proving the identity of a person.

Intimate Samples

Dental impression

-

Blood, Semen or Body Tissue Fluid

-

Urine

-

Pubic Hair

-

Swab from any part of a person's genitals

-

Swab from a body orifice other than the mouth

Taking an Intimate Sample

Dental Impression
-
Registered Dentist

Other Intimate Samples
-
Registered Medical Practitioner / Nurse / Paramedic

Urine
-
Not Specified

Authorisation to take Intimate Samples

A sample may be taken from a person in police detention
ONLY
if the Inspector or above has RGB the sample will tend to

```
          |
   ┌──────┴──────┐
confirm        disprove
```

involvement in a RECORDABLE offence

Authority in Terrorism cases?

⬇

Superintendent

| Suspect's Written Consent is Required |

DNA Screening
- Is for the purposes of elimination and requires only the person's consent e.g. testing a specific area for a serial rapist.

Ages & Consent
- As per fingerprints:
    - Under 14 / Parent or Guardian.
    - 14 – 16 / Parent or Guardian *and* Child.

Information to Suspect
- Authorisation given.
- Grounds including nature of the offence the person is suspected of committing.
- Subject to speculative search.
- Refusal without good cause *may* harm case if it comes to trial.
- Where the suspect is in police detention *or* at the police station voluntarily the officer *shall* also explain the right to legal advice.

- Information to be recorded including that the suspect consented.

Terrorism Act 2000
- Increases the authority to Superintendent for those persons detained under this legislation.
- Rather than prove disprove etc, this applies to being concerned in commission, preparation or instigation of an act of terrorism.

Q. What if the person is NOT in police station?
A. Where 2 or more non-intimate samples have been taken and although suitable proved to be insufficient, an *Inspector or above* may authorise an INTIMATE to be taken.

Q. What about a person CONVICTED of an offence outside England & Wales?
A. If a Qualifying Offence in England & Wales and 2 or more non-intimate samples have been taken and proved insufficient, an Inspector or above may authorise an INTIMATE sample to be taken to assist in the prevention OR detection of crime.

Insufficient Non-Intimate Samples
- In both instances the written consent of the suspect is still required.

HOWEVER

- If the offence took place outside of England and Wales then the Inspector *must* be satisfied that that taking the sample is necessary to *assist in the prevention OR detection of crime* so not tending to ***confirm or disprove involvement in a recordable offence.***
- Likewise there's no mention of the non-intimate samples being SUITABLE, simply INSUFFICIENT.
- Unlike the time frames for attending a police station for fingerprints/non-intimate samples to be taken after arrest, report, charge, conviction etc, there are NO time limits for either of these two scenarios.

Q. Will DNA evidence alone be sufficient for a conviction?
A. No, unless it can be shown the depositing of the DNA was clearly undertaken during the commission of a crime.

Q. When comparing DNA bands from the suspect to those found at the crime scene what will the prosecution seek to show from an evidential perspective?
A. The PROBABILITY of a match happening by chance & the LIKELIHOOD that the person responsible was in fact the defendant.

Q. Are Jurys allowed to consider PARTIAL or INCOMPLETE profiles?
A. Yes, subject to the Jury being made aware of the limitations and given sufficient evidence to evaluate it.

R v Bates (2006)
- The courts will allow juries to consider partial or incomplete DNA profiles subject to them being informed of the inherent limitations and provided sufficient information to provide an informed judgement such as he in which a 1:610,000 probability of a match was sufficient to support a conviction for murder.

R v Gabriel and Others (2020)
- Where DNA found on the muzzle of an uzi sub machine gun believed to be part of a conspiracy belonged to one of 3 monozygotic triplets, further evidenced linked to the use of a mobile phone and cell-site analysis was required to support the conviction.

R v FNC (2015)
- The requirement for supporting evidence is reduced, not obviated where for example, the defendant ejaculated onto the victim's trousers, an act clearly undertaken during the commission of a crime as opposed to for example...

- **R v Lashley (2000)** where DNA found on a half smoked cigarette at the scene of a robbery (behind the post office counter) required additional information. Here DNA only matched 7 out of 10 males in the UK which coupled with evidence of Lashley living or with connections in the area made the case compelling for the jury.

GENERAL PRINCIPLES
POLICE POWERS & PROCEDURES

SESSION 4

INTERVIEWS

What is an Interview

An interview is the questioning of a person regarding

- involvement
- suspected involvement

in a criminal offence

under

CAUTION

⬇

In general an interview of a person under arrest should take place at a police station or other authorised place of detention unless the consequent delay would be likely to

| Will lead to **INTERFERENCE** with or harm to evidence connected to an offence or interference with or physical harm to other people | Will hinder the recovery of **PROPERTY** from the offence | Will lead to the **ALERTING** of others suspected of the offence and not yet arrested for it |

&

Serious loss of or damage to property

R v McGuiness (1999)
- States that if a person is asked questions for reasons *other than obtaining evidence about his/her involvement or suspected involvement in an offence*, this is NOT an interview and a caution need not be given.

R v Miller (1998)
- The court held that asking the single question 'are these ecstasy tablets?' criminally implicated the person and therefore constituted an interview. This is very different to asking 'What is in the package?' when conducting a search.

Whelan v DPP (1995)
- A police officer, without caution, asked questions of a person sitting in the drivers seat of the stationary car with the key in the ignition to establish whether the person had been drinking and driven to that spot. The officer then requested a BT BUT this process did NOT constitute an interview as the commission of the offence did not arise until after the +ve BT and the caution was administered.

R v Wyna (2000)
- Contrast this to R v Wyna (2000) where a surveillance operation saw the suspect place a package in the boot of his car (4kg Heroin) and then later stopped him for speeding, the courts held that the subsequent conversation and alleged innocent explanation concerning possession of the package should have been conducted under caution when in fact it was not!

Note
- The inclusion of *serious loss of or damage to property*.
- Questioning will cease once the relevant risk has been averted.
- Suggested question could involve the journey to the police station where the DP shouts out of the window to his mate to let his associate know he's been arrested.

SO

- In this instance it will be okay to question the DP on the basis he/she may be *alerted*.

HOWEVER

- Watch out for the time schedule re the *recovery* for example, if the question talks about an offence that occurred a month ago for which your DP has just been arrested then this area is unlikely to be relevant.

Refusal to enter or remain in an Interview Room
- The codes allow the CO to authorise the interview to take place in the cell using portable recording equipment *or* if such equipment is not available, in writing.

Questions which do NOT amount to an Interview

Those which are asked solely to establish

Identity

Ownership of a vehicle

Statutory Requirement

Furtherance of a Search

Seek verification of a written record

Conducting and Recording Interviews

Visual Recordings

⬇

Discretion of Interviewing Officer

EXCEPT

for

| Interviews of Persons detained under s.41 or Schedule 7 Terrorism Act 2000 | Post-Charge questioning of persons detained under s.22 Counter Terrorism Act 2008 |

Pre Interview Disclosure

Will depend on the circumstances of the case and normally include

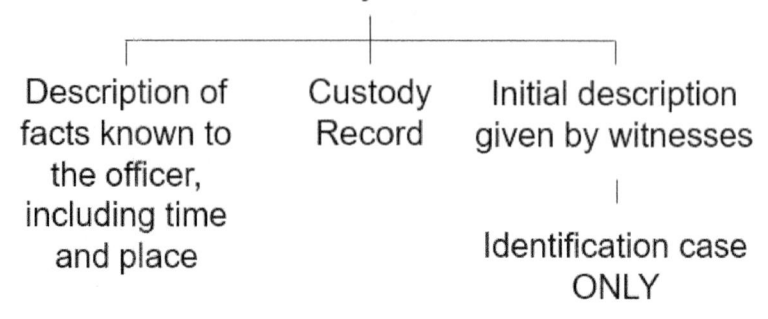

- Description of facts known to the officer, including time and place
- Custody Record
- Initial description given by witnesses
  - Identification case ONLY

Note
- This is a minimum requirement.
- Although the initial 'first' description shall, where practicable, be given to the suspect or solicitor before an identification procedure, this need NOT apply at the interview stage, ahead of any identification procedure.

R v Argent (1997)
- Dismissed argument that an inference could be NOT be drawn from a failure to provide full pre interview disclosure, although it would be a factor for the jury to consider when deciding whether the failure to answer questions was reasonable.

R v Hoare (2004)
- Legal advice alone to say nothing could NOT preclude the drawing of an adverse inference.

R v Thirlwell (2002)
- Officers may choose not to draw an inference from silence where disclosure of key evidence ahead of time may impact negatively on their case e.g. in this instance they chose not to disclose medical evidence re the possible causes of death at a murder trial and thereby give the defendant time to avoid implicating himself.

Interview without Legal Advice
Superintendent Authority

Where a Superintendent has reasonable grounds for believing that delay will lead to

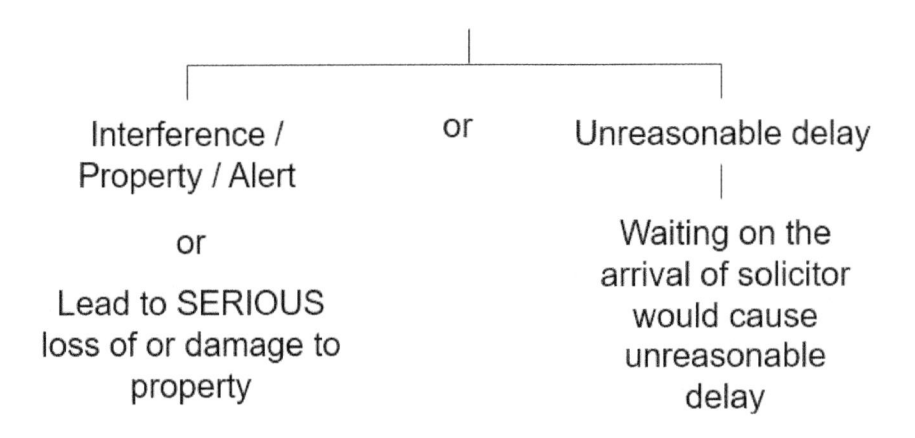

- Interference / Property / Alert

  or

  Lead to SERIOUS loss of or damage to property

or

- Unreasonable delay

  Waiting on the arrival of solicitor would cause unreasonable delay

QUESTION

Police Constable CHAHAL is covering the front office when he is approached by BILEY who states that he has stabbed his wife. PC CHAHAL arrests BILEY and rushes him through into the custody centre where BILEY demands to see a solicitor.

Given these circumstances, will it be possible to interview BILEY without him having received legal advice?

A. Yes, subject to an inspector or above having reasonable grounds for *suspecting* failure to interview BILEY will lead to physical injury.
B. Yes, subject to an inspector or above having reasonable grounds for *believing* failure to interview BILEY will lead to physical injury.
C. Yes, subject to a superintendent having reasonable grounds for *suspecting* failure to interview BILEY will lead to physical injury.
D. Yes, subject to a superintendent having reasonable grounds for *believing* failure to interview BILEY will lead to physical injury.

Answer D. Yes, subject to a superintendent having reasonable grounds for believing failure to interview BILEY will lead to physical injury, the interference element of this scenario relating to the ongoing or worsening of the physical injury to BILEY's wife.

Note
- While the custody record *must* be endorsed, it need *not* be by the Supt covering this area but by any Supt, unlike where there are disputes over Reviews.

Unreasonable Delay
- Regard should be given to how long the person has to remain in custody and the length of time it will take a solicitor to arrive.
- In the event of the time taken by the solicitor to arrive and the time left of the detention clock being at odds, the solicitor should be told in order that he might have another solicitor, nearer at hand to attend the police station on their behalf.

When should the interview stop?
- When the risk is adverted.

Q. Where a solicitor arrives in the middle of the interview, can he/she be allowed access to the client?
A. Yes, unless this would present an immediate risk of harm to people. (see Code C para 6.6(b)(i).

Adverse inferences
- Cannot be drawn from silence in this instance.

Interview without legal advice
Inspector

Where the solicitor nominated

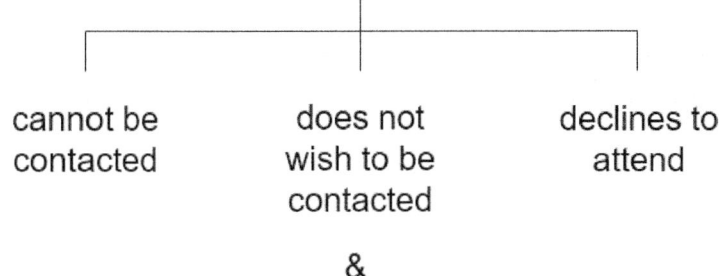

- cannot be contacted
- does not wish to be contacted
- declines to attend

&

has declined the duty solicitor

an Inspector **MAY** give permission to proceed

Note
- In this instance, adverse inference from silence will apply and as such the DP must be cautioned accordingly.

Interview without legal advice
'Change of Mind'

An Inspector or above

having enquired into his reasons

MAY

give permission to proceed

and the interviewee must agree in writing OR recording

Live Link Interviews
Inspectors Authority

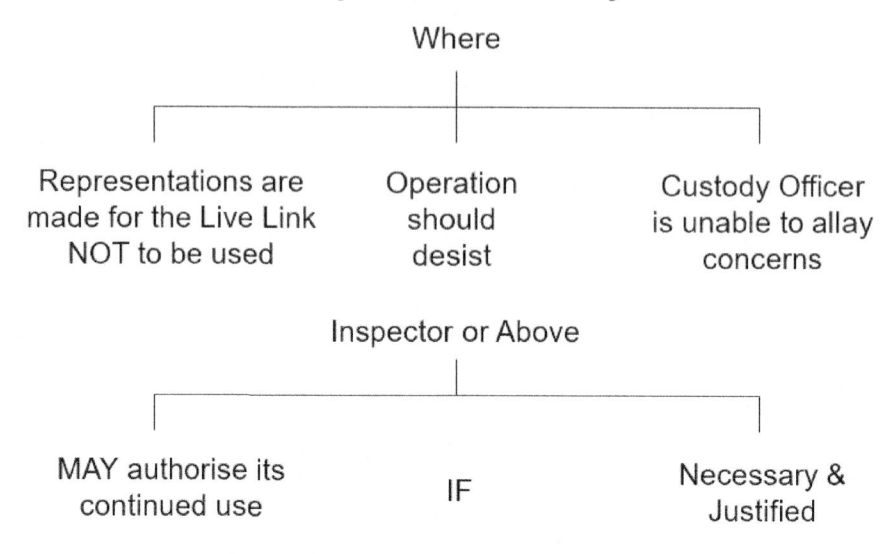

Where

- Representations are made for the Live Link NOT to be used
- Operation should desist
- Custody Officer is unable to allay concerns

Inspector or Above

- MAY authorise its continued use
- IF
- Necessary & Justified

Note
- When making this decision there are several things the Inspector must have regard to:
    - Circumstances of the suspect;
    - Nature & serious of the offence;
    - Impact on suspect & victim;
    - Representations of the Solicitor or AA;
    - Impact on the investigation by making the suspect be present for the interview;
    - Risk to evidential value e.g. if an interpreter is not present;
    - Likely impact due to the delay in arranging for an interpreter to be present.

Urgent Interviews
Vulnerable Suspects

Where an interview is to take place at a

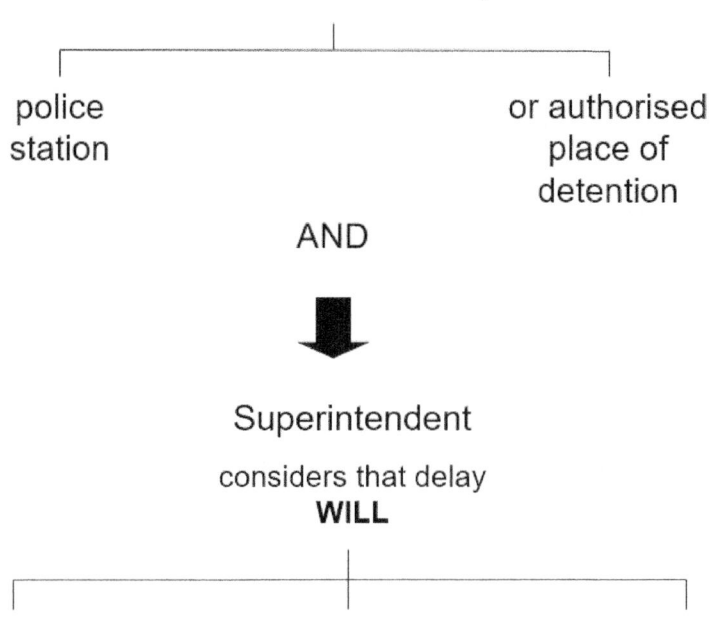

| police station | or authorised place of detention |

AND

⬇

Superintendent

considers that delay
WILL

| lead to **INTERFERENCE** with or harm to evidence connected to an offence or interference with or physical harm to other people | hinder the recovery of **PROPERTY** from the offence | lead to the **ALERTING** of others suspected of the offence and not yet arrested for it |

SERIOUS loss of or damage to property

⬇

then

the following persons may be interviewed

Drink/Drugs/Illness	**Juveniles**	**Language**
Unable to appreciate significance of Q&As or understand due to the influence of drink, drugs or illness	Juveniles, the mentally disordered or mentally vulnerable	Persons with difficulties with English / Hearing
MAY	**MAY**	**MAY**
be interviewed in that state	be interviewed without appropriate adult	be interviewed without an interpreter

Questioning must cease when sufficient information is obtained to avert the immediate risk

Interviews at Educational Establishments

Should only take place in exceptional circumstances with the agreement of the PRINCIPLE

The principle may become the appropriate adult if waiting for the parents or other AA would cause unreasonable delay

⬇

unless the juvenile is suspected of an offence directed at his/her educational establishment

Does not require consent of parents

When can a person be interviewed AFTER charge or having been informed they may be prosecuted?

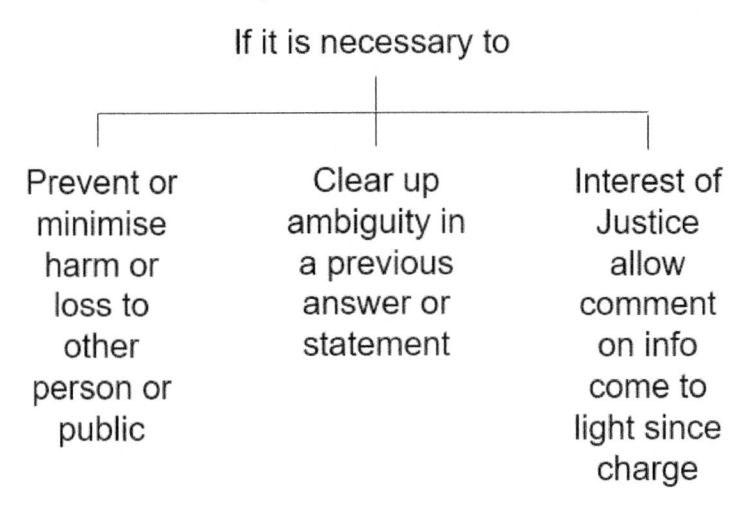

If it is necessary to

| Prevent or minimise harm or loss to other person or public | Clear up ambiguity in a previous answer or statement | Interest of Justice allow comment on info come to light since charge |

Note
- Old style caution must be used in this instance as no inferences may be drawn from these interviews i.e. no restriction on the right to silence.
- If done *contemporaneously* the DP should sign the forms or if refuses the *interviewing officer* & *any thirds parties* present should sign the forms.
- If *tape recorded* & the DP or any third party refuses to sign the label then Code E (para 4.15) requires an *inspector or above* or if not available the *custody officer* to sign it.

Notice of Intended Prosecutions (NIP)
- Service of an NIP does NOT amount to informing someone they will be prosecuted for an offence and so does not preclude them from further questioning.

Who may exclude a Solicitor from an Interview ?

If the investigating officer considers that a solicitor is acting in a way that he is UNABLE TO PROPERLY PUT QUESTIONS TO THE SUSPECT he will

⬇

stop the interview

⬇

and consult a Superintendent OR ABOVE

If not available?

⬇

an Inspector OR ABOVE will decide whether or not to exclude the solicitor from the interview.

What does a solicitor mean?
- A solicitor holding a current licence.
- A trainee solicitor.
- Duty solicitor representative or Accredited / Probationary representative

Unacceptable conduct by solicitor?
- Includes answering questions on the clients behalf and providing written replies for him to quote.

Speak to the Solicitor in question?
- Yes and then decide in the presence of that solicitor.

Consult with an other Solicitor
- Clearly this would be the case given these circumstances.

Report to the Law Society
- Consideration will be given so to do by the **Supt or above** making this decision at their discretion. It is not definite so watch out for the must in the question!

QUESTION

Who reports the facts to the superintendent

A. Interviewing officer.
B. Officer in the case.
C. Custody officer.
D. Inspector.

Answer D.

Special Warnings

When a suspect who is interviewed after arrest fails, refuses or answers unsatisfactorily certain questions after due warning a court or jury may draw inferences as appear proper

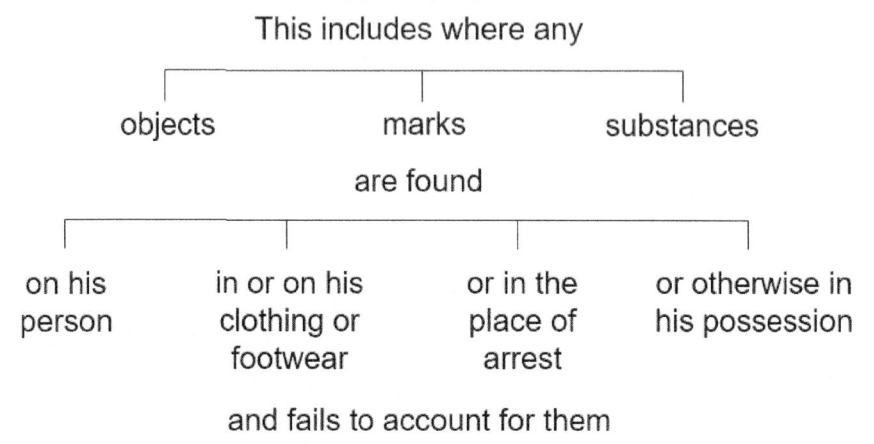

This includes where any

- objects
- marks
- substances

are found

- on his person
- in or on his clothing or footwear
- or in the place of arrest
- or otherwise in his possession

and fails to account for them

Note
- This can only take place after arrest so not for voluntary interviews.

These provisions also apply to any questions about why the suspect was

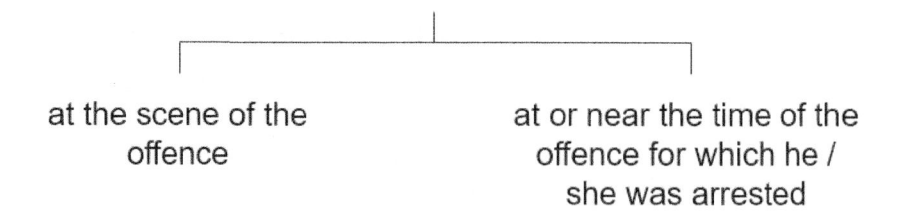

- at the scene of the offence
- at or near the time of the offence for which he / she was arrested

and fails or refuses to account for his/her presence at or near the scene of the offence

It must be made clear to the suspect what matters he/she is being asked to answer and the consequences of remaining silent on EACH OCCASION.

QUESTION

LEE is seen by PC CLARKE exiting the ground floor window of a house at 3am in the morning. LEE runs off when challenged by PC Clarke and disappears into a nearby housing estate. PC Clarke circulates his description and shortly after, LEE is detained and arrested on suspicion of burglary by PC NOAH. During the subsequent interview PC NOAH questions LEE regarding his presence at the scene of the burglary, to which LEE makes no comment.

In respect of these circumstances can PC NOAH administer a special warning to LEE?

A. Yes, PC NOAH is entitled to administer a special warning to LEE as he was seen by PC CLARKE at the scene of the burglary.
B. Yes, as PC NOAH arrested LEE in direct response to PC CLARKE's circulation the special warning may be administered.
C. No, as PC NOAH was not the officer who saw LEE at the scene of the burglary he cannot administer the special warning.
D. No, PC NOAH would only be able to administer the special warning if PC CLARKE was also present during LEE's interview

Answer C.

An officer can administer the special warning so long as the arresting officer is the same as the officer who saw the offender at the scene. In this case however, we have a different officer who saw the offender at the scene (PC Clarke), to that of the arresting officer (PC Noah). Therefore, neither PC Noah nor indeed any officer is able to administer a special warning in these circumstances.

Note
- This requirement does not however apply were LEE to have been found in possession of any mark, object substance etc at the time of arrest

Special Warning

WORDING

In ORDINARY language

What offence is being investigated

-

What fact the suspects is being asked to account for

-

That the interviewing officer BELIEVES this fact may be due to the suspect having taken part in the offence

-

That a court may draw a proper inference if the suspect fails or refuses to account for the fact being questioned

-

That a record is being made of the interview and it MAY be given in evidence at any subsequent trial

Note
- The special warning must be administered for each relevant question.

Breaks from Interview

Should be made at recognised mealtimes (min 45mins)

Short refreshment breaks after 2 hours should last at least 15 mins

May be delayed at the interviewing officer's discretion where there are reasonable grounds for believing that it would

- involve risk or harm to people or serious loss of or damage to property
- delay unnecessarily the person's release from custody
- otherwise prejudice the outcome of the investigation

recorded, with grounds, during interview

Rest Periods

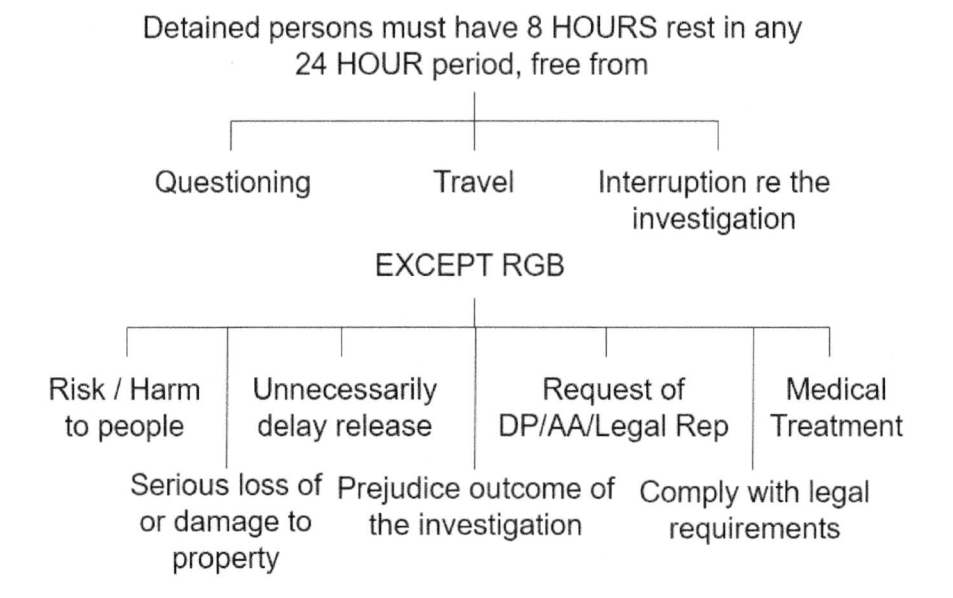

Detained persons must have 8 HOURS rest in any 24 HOUR period, free from

- Questioning
- Travel
- Interruption re the investigation

EXCEPT RGB

- Risk / Harm to people
- Unnecessarily delay release
- Request of DP/AA/Legal Rep
- Medical Treatment
- Serious loss of or damage to property
- Prejudice outcome of the investigation
- Comply with legal requirements

Note
- In the case of:
    - Risk / Harm to people;
    - Serious loss of or damage to property;
    - Unnecessarily delay release;
    - Prejudice outcome of the investigation;

ONLY in each of these instances, a FRESH period to be allowed.

Unsolicited Comments which might be Relevant to an Offence

'Significant Statements'

A WRITTEN record shall be made, which should:

- be timed & signed by the maker

- where practicable, the person should be given the opportunity to read it & to sign it as correct

 or

- to indicate where he considers it inaccurate

 &

- any refusal to sign shall be recorded

Note
Significant Statements can only be made to:
- Police Officers;
- Police Staff.

Bately v DPP (1998)
- Held that the endorsement was *not required immediately* & there was nothing to constrain the police from returning the next day to get this endorsement.

Bits and Bobs

Where a DP Refuses to sign the Interview Tape Label an Inspector or above MUST sign it or if not available the custody officer

---

Where it is necessary to break the seal on a master tape this MUST be done in the presence of a representative of the CPS

Significant statements or silences should be put to the DP at the beginning of the interview after caution and ask whether he/she confirms or denies the statement or wishes to add anything

---

If the person being interviewed cannot read then the **person taking the statement** shall read it to him & ask whether he/she would like to correct, alter or add anything & put his/her signature or mark at the end

Break Seal on Master Tape
- The defendant or legal rep should be give *reasonable opportunity to attend* & if they do be invited to re seal & sign the master tape.

Person making a statement cannot read
- The officer shall then certify what has happened.

GENERAL PRINCIPLES
POLICE POWERS & PROCEDURES

SESSION 5

RELEASE OF PERSONS ARRESTED

Power of Arrest
'Failure to Answer Police Bail'

A constable may arrest without warrant any person who

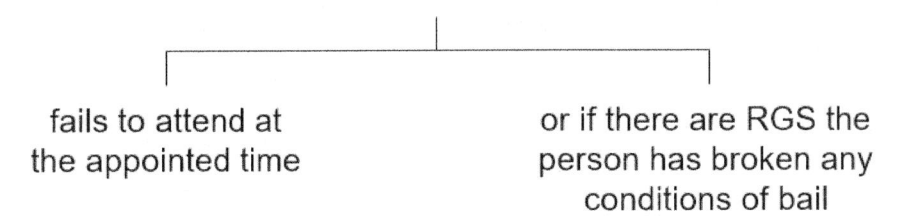

- fails to attend at the appointed time
- or if there are RGS the person has broken any conditions of bail

Pre-Charge Bail Restrictions
'Terrorist Offences'

A person commits an offence if

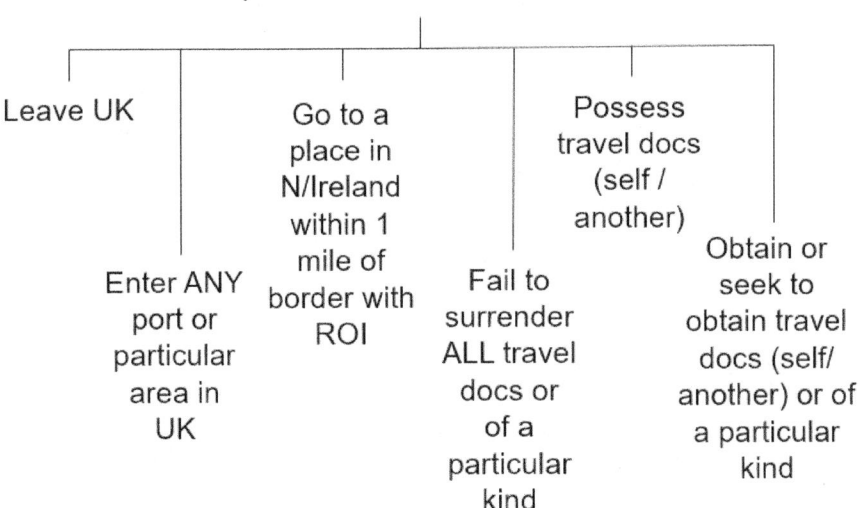

- Leave UK
- Enter ANY port or particular area in UK
- Go to a place in N/Ireland within 1 mile of border with ROI
- Fail to surrender ALL travel docs or of a particular kind
- Possess travel docs (self / another)
- Obtain or seek to obtain travel docs (self/ another) or of a particular kind

Note
- Travel docs include passports (UK or Otherwise).
- Includes ATTEMPTS.

Bail Restrictions

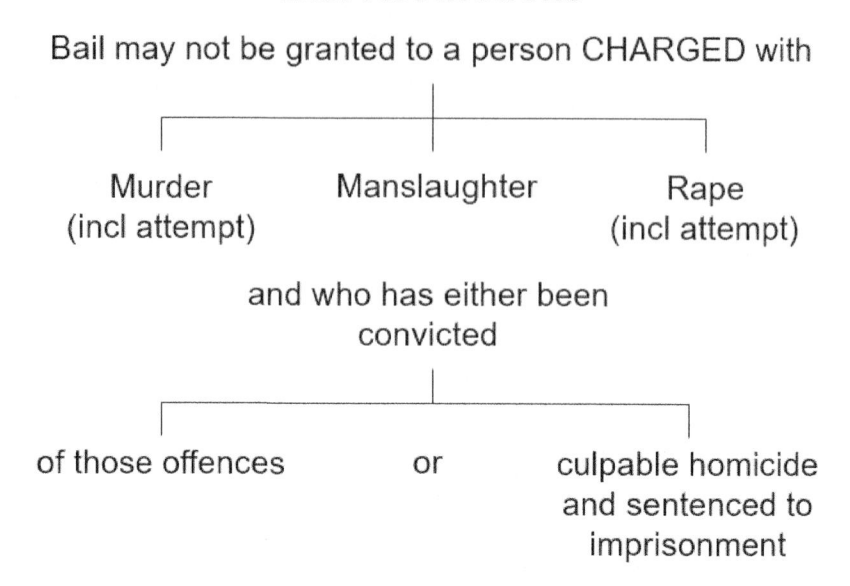

Bail may not be granted to a person CHARGED with

- Murder (incl attempt)
- Manslaughter
- Rape (incl attempt)

and who has either been convicted

- of those offences
- or
- culpable homicide and sentenced to imprisonment

unless there are exceptional circumstances

Note
- This extends to Assault by penetration (including causing another to engage in sexual activity without consent where penetration was involved) and sexual offences relating to children and those persons with mental disorders which *impede choice*.
- In the case of a person previously convicted of Manslaughter or Culpable Homicide (Scotland) Bail MAY be granted if they were NOT sentenced to imprisonment or if he was a child or young person, to long term detention under any of the above unless one of the grounds to refuse bail under S38 PACE apply.

Hurnam v State of Mauritius (2005)
- Seriousness of the offence is NOT a conclusive reason for refusing bail and the court must consider whether or not the accused is likely to abscond.

Grounds for the Refusal of Bail

A custody officer must grant bail to a person (Adult) charged with an offence unless RGB

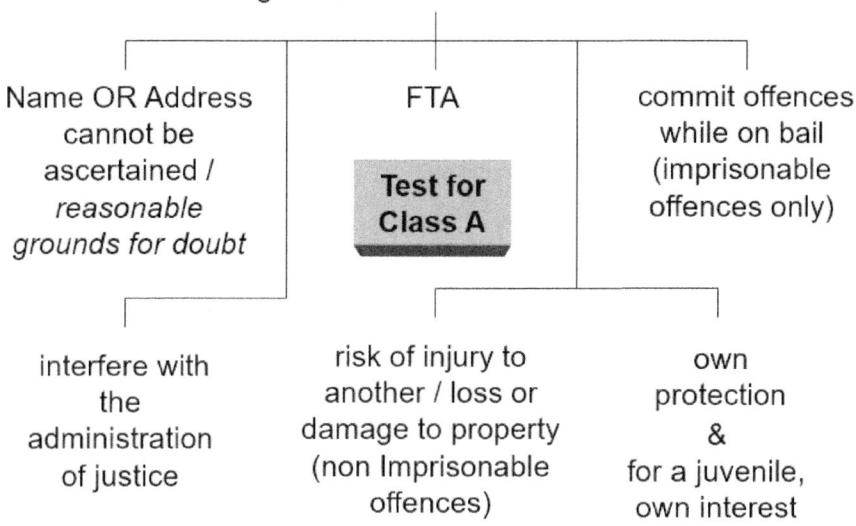

- Name OR Address cannot be ascertained / *reasonable grounds for doubt*
- FTA — **Test for Class A**
- commit offences while on bail (imprisonable offences only)
- interfere with the administration of justice
- risk of injury to another / loss or damage to property (non Imprisonable offences)
- own protection & for a juvenile, own interest

Note
- Applies to 1 or more.

Name or Address
- If the person refuses to give their name this does *not* automatically satisfy this requirement as the actual wording says Name **or** Address cannot be ascertained or *that which is given is doubted*.

ALSO

- There is a difference between 'not knowing' the name or address and 'cannot be ascertained' so watch out for this in a question.

Except for Name and Address
- Factors for consideration by both the CO and the Court include:
    - Nature & seriousness of the offence;
    - Character, antecedents, associations & community ties;
    - Previous record for having FTA;

- Strength of evidence (but not for cases adjourned for inquiries or reports);
- Substantial grounds for causing physical / mental harm to others including a person associated with the accused (domestic violence issue)

ALSO

- Neither the COURT nor the CO need grant bail (Imprisonable only) where there are **SUBSTANTIAL** grounds for believing:
  - FTA custody;
  - Commit an offence;
  - Interfere with witnesses or otherwise obstruct course of justice re him/her or otherwise.

Commit further Offences
- Requires the CO to give due weight to the above and whether the accused has *previously offended on bail.*

Interfere with Administration of Justice
- For example, witness inference, but not for the purpose of the police making further enquiries or where further suspects are to be arrested.

Risk of Injury
- Detention necessary to prevent accused causing physical injury to another OR causing loss or damage to property but NOT serious loss or damage.

Own protection
- Can relate to protection from themselves e.g. suicidal, alcoholic, drug addition, mental instability OR protect from others such as child abusers where there is a lot of public anger directed at the suspect.

Juvenile own welfare
- Applies to *under 17 years* with a wider meaning to include homelessness, prostitution or vagrancy.

QUESTION

Having charged GARDOT with multiple cases of fraud the custody officer is discussing the issue of bail with Detective Constable JACKMAN, the arresting officer. DC JACKMAN is of the opinion that should GARDOT be bailed he would liquidate his assets to travel aboard and in so doing become a flight risk. As there remain ongoing enquiries however, the officer does not want the source of this information disclosed.

Given these circumstances which of the following statements is correct?

A. Should bail be refused, the source of the information giving rise to the officer's opinion must be disclosed to GARDOT.
B. Should bail be refused, the source of the information giving rise to the officer's opinion need not be disclosed to GARDOT.
C. Should GARDOT be refused bail, authorisation not to disclose the source of the information must come from an Inspector or above.
D. Should GARDOT be refused bail, authorisation not to disclose the source of the information must come from a Superintendent or above.

Answer B.

his question relates to R (on the application of Ajaib) v Birmingham Magistrates' Court in which it was held that the officers opinion in circumstances similar to those in this question were sufficient for the source of the information not to be disclosed.

Bail Conditions

Conditions may be imposed by a custody officer if it appears necessary to prevent the person from

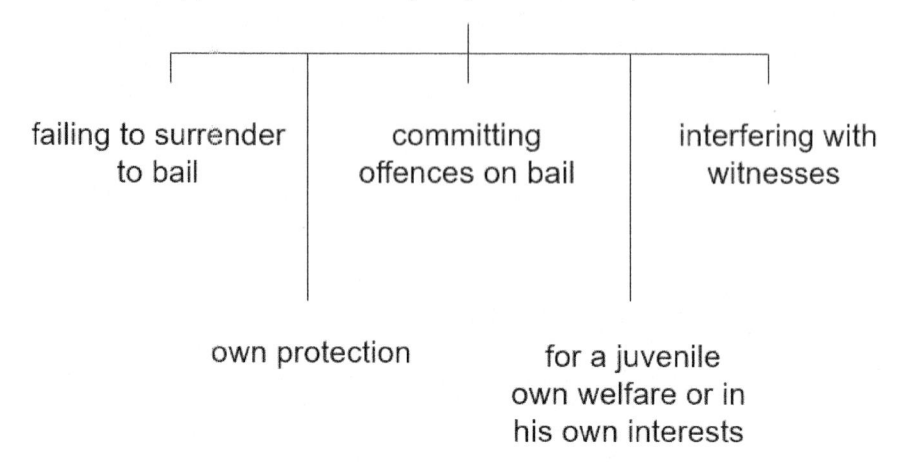

- failing to surrender to bail
- committing offences on bail
- interfering with witnesses
- own protection
- for a juvenile own welfare or in his own interests

Bail Conditions

Where a custody officer decides to grant bail, one or more conditions can be imposed

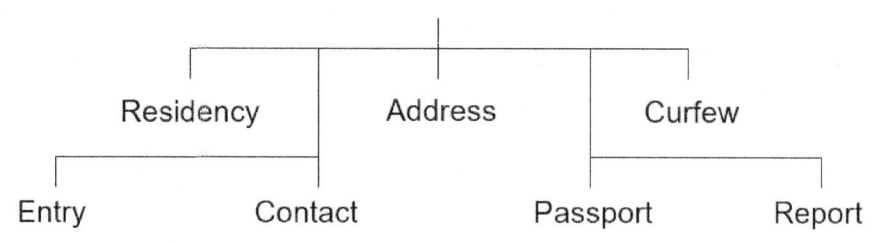

- Residency
- Address
- Curfew
- Entry
- Contact
- Passport
- Report

Residency
- Live and sleep at the same address.

Address
- To notify any changes of address.

Curfew
- At set times i.e. when likely to commit offences even when only allowed out for 2 hours each day (**McDonald v Procurator Fiscal, Elgin 2003**) i.e. must be proportionate.

Entry
- Not to enter specified buildings or addresses or go within a specified distance of the premises.

Contact
- Not to contact a specific person e.g. victim, prosecution witness.

Passport
- To surrender where, as with the above conditions, there is a **real risk** of the person absconding.

Report
- To report to a police station (daily, weekly or at other intervals).
- Can also be applied by a constable granting bail elsewhere that a police station.

Varying Bail Conditions
- May be done by the CO who first granted bail OR any other CO *serving at the same police station* at the request of the bailee BUT in so doing may impose further conditions or more onerous conditions.

Electronic monitoring
- CO does not have authority to bail for electronic monitoring of a juvenile or young person.
- This is an *option for the court* subject to the person being *12 years or over* and charged with an offence of a violent or sexual nature or were the child an adult to have committed an offence with a term of imprisonment of 14 years:
    - To a bail or probation hostel;
    - For court reports;
    - Medical reports.

R (on application of Carson) v Ealing Mags Court (2012)
- This case involved the serious racially aggravated harassment of Carson's neighbour who was given a pre-charge *bail condition not to reside at her home*.
- This decision was upheld at Magistrates' Court, but with no right of Appeal in such instances, a judicial review to the High Court found this *decision to be disproportionate* on the basis that Carson had not been charged with the offence, had not seen the evidence against her and the length of time before any potential trial.

R v Bournemouth Magistrates' Court (1989)
- This case identified that in relation to a non-imprisonable offence of s.5 Public Order Act (Disorderly Behaviour) by a hunt protester, a bail condition was *correctly given for the person not to attend another hunt meeting before his next court appearance*.

Refusal of Bail

Where bail is refused the detained person MUST be told as soon as possible unless

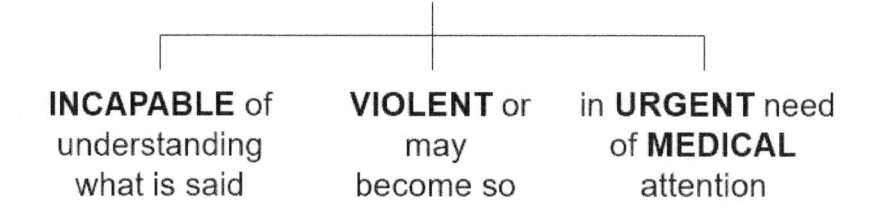

| **INCAPABLE** of understanding what is said | **VIOLENT** or may become so | in **URGENT** need of **MEDICAL** attention |

Sureties

A court or custody officer, when granting bail may require 1 or more sureties to secure the defendant to bail

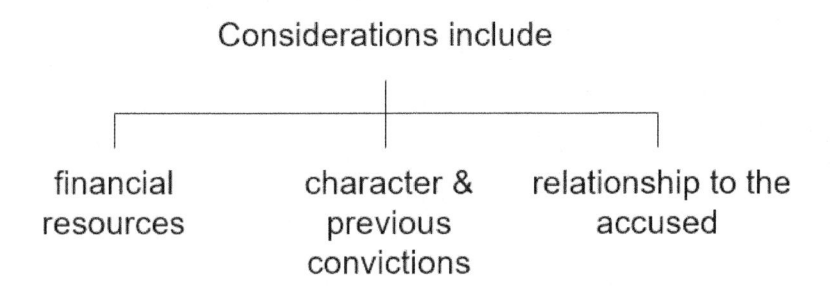

Considerations include

- financial resources
- character & previous convictions
- relationship to the accused

Note
- In cases of failure to surrender to bail, the surety *may* be required unless they *took all reasonable steps to ensure the surrender to bail* which includes *notification to a constable in writing*.
- A DP may NOT stand as his/her own surety.

QUESTION

Where a person is bailed and he/she goes on to commit further offences or interfere with witnesses while on bail, will the surety be forfeited?

A. Yes.
B. No.

Answer B. No, as the purpose of a surety is for the person to surrender to custody and not to prevent further offences taking place.

QUESTION

Who decides the suitability of an individual surety?

A. Custody Officer.

B. Inspector or above.

Answer A.

QUESTION

Where a suitable surety is unavailable, who can fix the amount of cash or security required to fulfil this requirement?

A. Custody Officer.
B. Inspector or above.

Answer A. The security can as inferred by this question be cash or some other valuable item deemed suitable by the custody officer and which can be forfeited in the event of non-attendance in answer to bail.

QUESTION

Can a third party make an asset available for security to secure the accused's release on bail?

A. Yes.
B. No.

Answer A.

QUESTION

Having appeared in Magistrates' Court for an offence of Fraud (Abuse of Position) CARROLE is unable to secure a surety for her release on bail.

Which of the following circumstances correctly identifies how this situation may be addressed?

A. The recognisance of the surety may only be entered into before the court officer.
B. The recognizance of the surety may later be entered into before a custody officer.

C. The recognizance of the surety may later be entered into before an Inspector or above.
D. The recognizance of the surety may later be entered into before an Inspector or above, an officer in charge of the station or other specified person.

Answer D.

Other specified person refers to the court officer, the defendant's custodian where the defendant is in custody, which in this case is an Inspector or above or the officer in charge of the police station or someone acting with the authority of either.

Juveniles Refused Bail

Where a juvenile is **refused bail AFTER CHARGE** the custody officer shall make arrangements for him to be taken into the care of the local authority **unless**

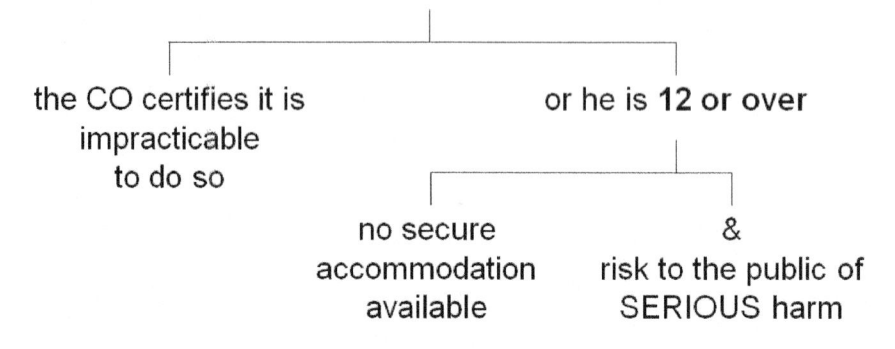

```
         the CO certifies it is                or he is 12 or over
            impracticable
              to do so
                                          no secure            &
                                       accommodation    risk to the public of
                                          available        SERIOUS harm
```

Monitored by an Inspector or Above

Note
- Taken into care of the local authority applies 24/7.
- Certificate must be produced to the court at the first appearance.
- Chief officers are required to ensure the operation of these procedures are monitored by an *Inspector or above*.
- Once charged bail *cannot* be refused simply on the grounds an AA is not available *unless* the absence of the adult provides the custody officer with the necessary grounds for authorising detention after charge.

QUESTION

CORK, a recidivist offender and frequent missing person from local authority care, is eleven years of age. At 2 a.m. on Monday morning he has been charged with the offence of arson with intent to endanger life and refused bail. Due to appear at Magistrates' Court later that morning, the custody officer decides to keep CORK in custody rather than transfer him into care of the local authority in readiness for that appearance.

Under which of the following circumstances will this decision be correct?

A. If the custody officer certifies it was impracticable for CORK to be taken into the care of the local authority.
B. If an Inspector or above certifies it was impracticable for CORK to be taken into the care of the local authority.
C. If the custody officer considered CORK represented a risk to the public of serious harm.
D. If an Inspector or above considered CORK represented a risk to the public of serious harm.

Answer A.
Given representing a risk to the public of serious harm ONLY applies to juveniles 12 years of age or over, this immediately discounts options C and D and of course the same would equally apply to a lack of secure accommodation were that to have been an option.

Now, although, local authority care applies 24/7, it is the issue of impracticability which applies here. It CANNOT however be based on the juveniles behaviour nor the nature of the offence. Nor is it about travel arrangements which might well have been a problem given these circumstances.

The key here therefore is about EXCEPTIONAL CIRCUMSTANCES which either render movement of the child impossible, perhaps a snowstorm, flood or something similar OR that the child is due to appear at court in a short time and as such would be deprived of rest OR miss the court appearance.

The only option therefore is to *certify* it was impracticable to transfer CORK into care of the local authority, the only remaining question being as to who signs the certificate and in this case it is the Custody Officer albeit with the proceedings in such cases being monitored by an Inspector or above.

Live Link Bail

Applies to a person required by a Magistrates' Court to engage in a preliminary hearing via live link from a police station

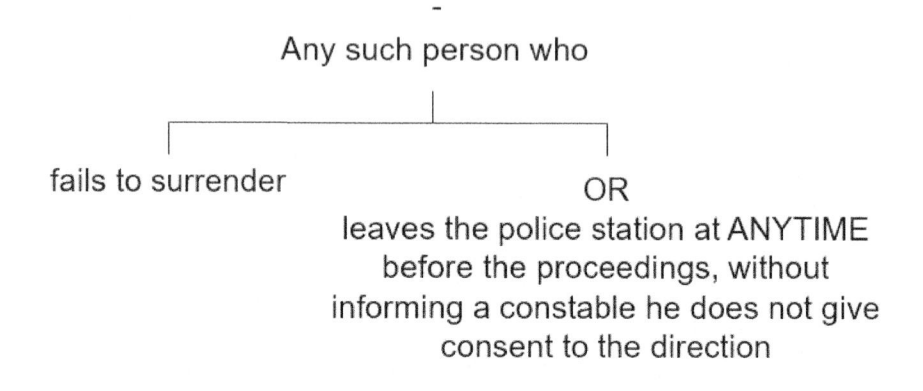

Any such person who

- **fails to surrender**

OR

- **leaves the police station at ANYTIME before the proceedings, without informing a constable he does not give consent to the direction**

may be arrested

Note
- Also applies to persons already in custody *however*, where a Live Link direction to attend a police station is given by the court, the person will be treated as *having surrendered to the court* and must therefore be seen and heard as if in court.

Live Link Bail

'Power to Search'

A person may be searched on arrival at the police station and items seized or cause to be seized if there are

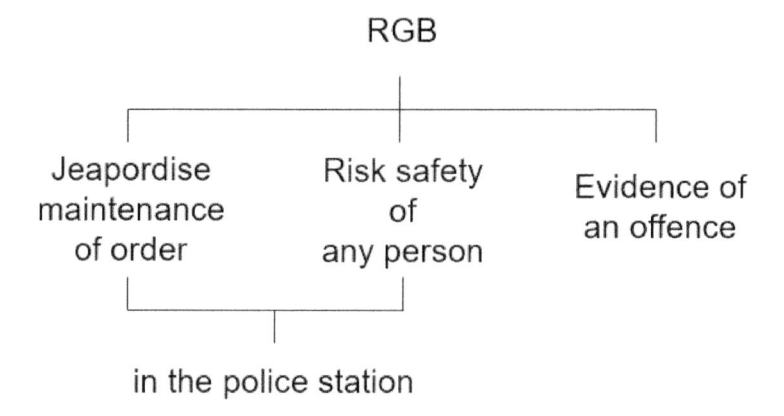

RGB

- Jeapordise maintenance of order
- Risk safety of any person
- Evidence of an offence

in the police station

Note
- Search does not extend to 'Intimate.'
- Same sex rules apply and refusal to be searched means the defendant can be arrested.

Power to Arrest for Absconding or Breaking Bail Conditions

'Court'

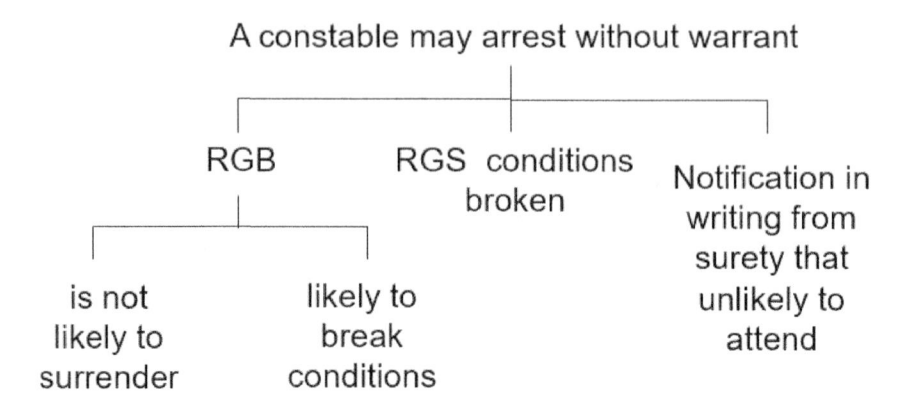

A constable may arrest without warrant

- **RGB**
  - is not likely to surrender
  - likely to break conditions
- **RGS conditions broken**
- **Notification in writing from surety that unlikely to attend**

Note

- The person must then be *brought before the 'Justice' within 24 hours of arrest*. So it's not good enough for the person to simply be at the court within 24 hours i.e. in the precinct, cells or even having been presented to the court advocate.
- This section merely confers a power of arrest and therefore is not an offence under the Bail Act.

Offence of Absconding by Persons Released on Bail

A person commits an offence who has been released on bail in criminal proceedings and fails to surrender

| without reasonable cause | OR | with reasonable cause as soon after the appointed time as reasonably practicable |

Applies to:

- police bail for suspect to appear at a police station
- police bail for defendant's 1st appearance at court
- court bail for defendant to return to court at a later date

Reasonably practicable
- Watch out for the question where the person is hospitalised at the time of surrender, but then once discharged either waits to attend court or doesn't bother.

Reasonable cause
- Getting the day wrong is not a reasonable.
- Nor is being a half hour late.

Q. What if the custody officer forgets to give the DP a copy of the bail sheet?
A. Not reasonable.

Remand in Police Custody

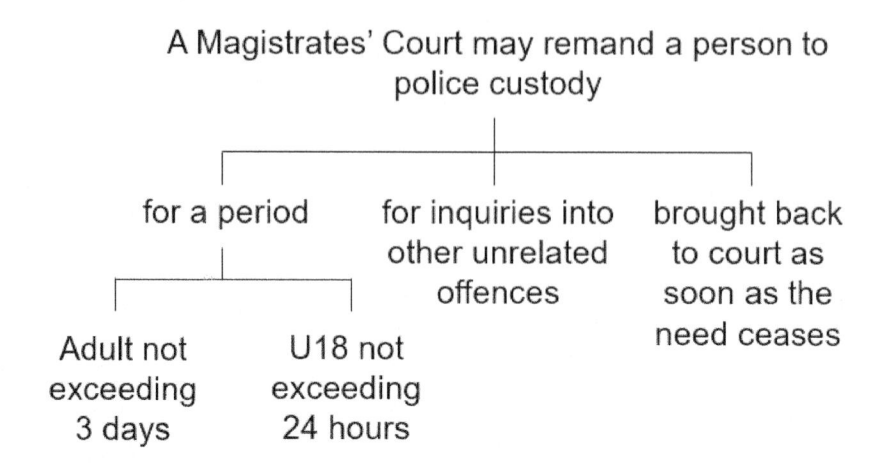

A Magistrates' Court may remand a person to police custody

- for a period
  - Adult not exceeding 3 days
  - U18 not exceeding 24 hours
- for inquiries into other unrelated offences
- brought back to court as soon as the need ceases

QUESTION

JAMES is in custody having committed a series of burglaries. At 2 p.m. he is charged with a number of offences and refused bail on the grounds that he may commit further offences if released from custody.

In accordance with Section 40 PACE 1984, which of the following statements is accurate in terms of JAMES review requirement?

A. JAMES's detention must be reviewed no later than 8 p.m. by the custody officer.
B. JAMES's detention must be reviewed no later than 11 p.m. by the custody officer.
C. JAMES's detention must be reviewed no later than 8 p.m. by an Inspector or above.
D. JAMES's detention must be reviewed no later than 11 p.m. by an Inspector or above

Answer B. A person who is refused Bail must still have his/her detention reviewed by the Custody Officer i.e. review after charge. This must take place within 9 hours of the last decision to refuse bail. *The same applies where a Magistrates' Court remands a person into police custody.*

GENERAL PRINCIPLES
POLICE POWERS & PROCEDURES

SESSION 6

DISCLOSURE OF EVIDENCE

Disclosure

Disclosure applies to material

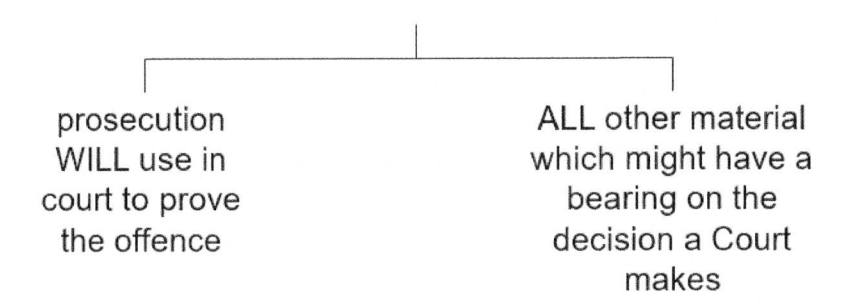

- prosecution WILL use in court to prove the offence
- ALL other material which might have a bearing on the decision a Court makes

Failure to Comply

Consequences of the prosecution failing to comply with their obligations include

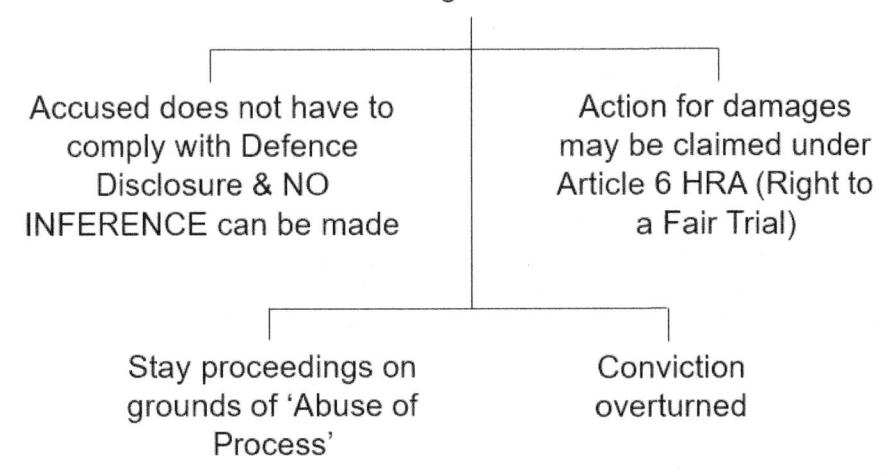

- Accused does not have to comply with Defence Disclosure & NO INFERENCE can be made
- Action for damages may be claimed under Article 6 HRA (Right to a Fair Trial)
- Stay proceedings on grounds of 'Abuse of Process'
- Conviction overturned

Criminal Investigation

Police officers or other persons have a duty to conduct an investigation to ascertain whether a person

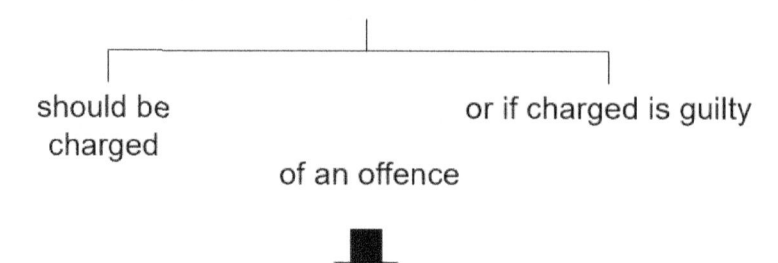

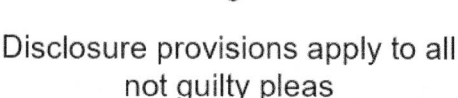

- should be charged
- or if charged is guilty

of an offence

⬇

Disclosure provisions apply to all not guilty pleas

CPS have responsibility for disclosure to the defence

Note
- Have a duty applies not only to police officers, but also those with a primary responsibility related to criminal offences e.g. Customs & excise and Benefit Agency Fraud investigators.
- The codes also say that in conducting an investigation, the investigator should pursue ALL reasonable lines of enquiry whether these point *towards or away from the suspect* (proportionate to the seriousness of the investigation) & retain all material, regardless of whether it is helpful to the prosecution or not i.e. could lead to a miscarriage of justice.

Preparation of Material for Prosecutor

The **disclosure officer** MUST ensure the appropriate schedule of unused material is prepared where the accused is charged with

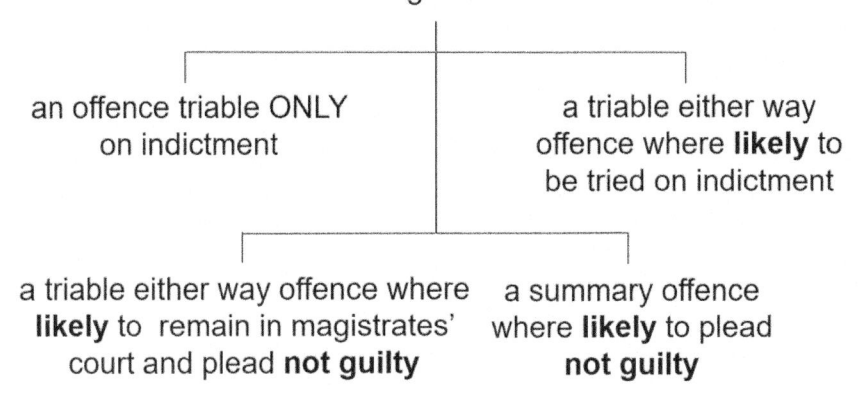

- an offence triable ONLY on indictment
- a triable either way offence where **likely** to be tried on indictment
- a triable either way offence where **likely** to remain in magistrates' court and plead **not guilty**
- a summary offence where **likely** to plead **not guilty**

Preparation of Material for Prosecutor

'Magistrates' Court'

Where the accused is charged with a

- summary offence
- or either-way offence likely to remain in a magistrates' court

AND
the anticipated plea is 'Guilty'
a Streamlined Disclosure Certificate (SDC)
is **not** required

Not Guilty plea
- An SDC must be completed.

Change of plea
- If the defendant changes his plea from G to NG, the Disclosure Officer must ensure the SDC is completed as soon as practicable so not with 3 days, 5 days, 7 days or whatever other options may appear in the answer to such a question.

SDC
- Where the SDC is not required, there is nonetheless a common law duty to disclose material which may assist the defence at a bail hearing or in the early preparation of the defendant's case e.g. key witness has previous convictions / witness has withdrawn his/her statement.

Preparation of Material for Prosecutor
'Crown Court'

Applies where the accused is charged with an offence

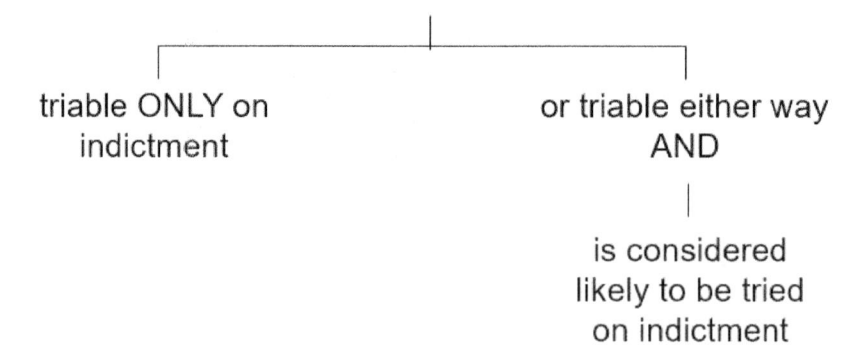

triable ONLY on indictment

or triable either way AND

is considered likely to be tried on indictment

Initial Disclosure

Prosecutor to disclose material to the defence, which might undermine the prosecution case against the accused or assist the case for the accused

or

provide a written statement that there is no such material

Sensitive Material

is disclosed to the prosecutor separately and includes that which the disclosure officer believes is

Not in the Public Interest to Disclose

Timeframe for Initial Disclosure
- ASAP after the duty arises i.e. there is no specific timeframe set.

Undermine the prosecution
- Case includes anything that tends to show a fact inconsistent with the elements of the case that must be proved by the prosecution:
    - Could be used in cross examination;
    - Support an exclusion of evidence / stay of proceedings / acted contrary to HRA;
    - Provide an explanation or partial explanation as to the accused's action.

Sensitive material includes:
- Confidential information;
- Observation posts;
- Informants;
- Police communications.

QUESTION

Who decides whether sensitive material should be disclosed to the Defence?

A. Officer in the case.
B. Disclosure Officer.
C. Prosecutor.
D. Judge.

Answer D via Public Interest Immunity (PII) application.

QUESTION

Where a PII Application fails, who makes the decision to abandon the case?

A. CPS Head of Dept & ACC or above.
B. DPP & ACC or above.

Answer A.

QUESTION

Under which of the following *exceptional* circumstances will sensitive material NOT be listed on the relevant documentation?

A. Where the *investigator* considers it inappropriate and would be likely to lead *directly* to loss of life or threaten national security.
B. Where the *investigator* considers it inappropriate and would be likely to lead *indirectly* to loss of life or threaten national security.
C. Where the *prosecutor* considers it inappropriate and would be likely to lead *directly* to loss of life or threaten national security.
D. Where the *prosecutor* considers it inappropriate and would be likely to lead *indirectly* to loss of life or threaten national security.

Answer A. The material must still be revealed to the prosecutor but separately from that of the relevant documentation.

QUESTION

COLE is a registered informant due to stand trial for murder. Concerned that this may come out during his trial he contacts his police handler, Detective Sergeant FARROW, who tells him not to tell his defence counsel about his status?

Has DS FARROW acted correctly in this instance?

A. Yes, as there is no duty for the Crown to disclose COLE's status to the Defence in these circumstances.
B. No, the Crown is required to seek a ruling from the Judge regarding COLE's status in these circumstances.

Answer A.
Given COLE is the defendant and knows he is an informant, it can therefore be safely assumed these circumstances have already been disclosed, therefore DS Farrow's advice is correct as in R v Denton (2002).

Disclosure by the Defence

Arises after Initial Disclosure

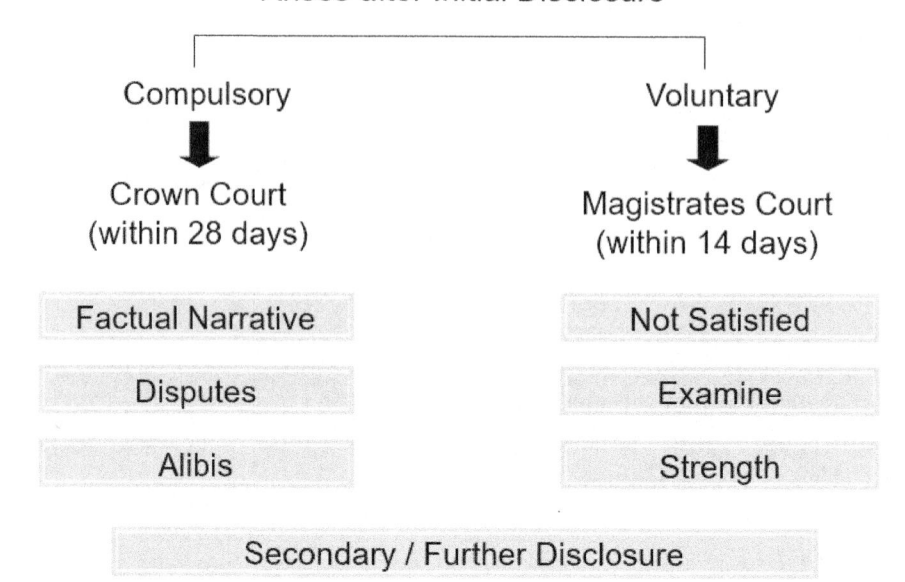

```
         Compulsory                    Voluntary
             ↓                             ↓
        Crown Court                  Magistrates Court
       (within 28 days)               (within 14 days)

       Factual Narrative                Not Satisfied

          Disputes                        Examine

           Alibis                         Strength

            Secondary / Further Disclosure
```

Note
- The duty of the defence to disclose arises AFTER the prosecution provides Initial Disclosure and may be Compulsory or Voluntary.
- The disclosure required by the defence is limited to material they intend to use at trial.

Compulsory Disclosure
- Does NOT *apply to Magistrates' Court* so ONLY at Crown Court and includes:
    - Set out the nature of the defence in general terms i.e. a *'factual narrative'* of their case;
    - Outline any *disputes* i.e. points of law (stops defence from going on fishing expeditions);
    - Outline any *alibis* e.g. Name / Address / *Date of Birth* of the alibi witness – there is no duty to disclose these details to a co-accused, although this could be done voluntarily.

Q. Can a Defence statement be made available to a co-accused?
A. Yes, applications may be made by co-accused(s) and the court will set the timeframe against which this requirement must be served.

Sanctions for failing to comply with Defence Statement requirements?
- With leave of the court ANY other party may make comment as appropriate;
- Court or jury may draw an INFERENCE regarding guilt (but requires other evidence to convict);
- If served outside of 14 days, consider need for further disclosure.

Voluntary
- Applies to cases being tried at Magistrates Court and happens where:
    - The defence are *not satisfied* with material disclosed at Initial Disclosure;
    - The defence wish to *examine* items listed in schedule of non-sensitive material;
    - Defence wish to show the prosecution the *strength* of their case in an attempt to persuade prosecution from proceeding.

Secondary Disclosure
- Once the defence statement has been provided the prosecution must, in both compulsory and voluntary cases, disclose any material:
    - Has not already been disclosed;
    - Which might reasonably be expected to *assist the accused's defence*.

Appeal Process
- Is available for the defence to apply for the prosecution to disclose further material after secondary disclosure.

Continuing Duty of Prosecution Disclosure

Prosecution must continue to review the disclosure of material in terms of whether it might undermine the prosecution case after

| compulsory | voluntary |

disclosure by the defence

Duty of Disclosure Officer

In addition to the provision of the various schedules the Disclosure Officer must also provide

| 1st Description | Explanation |
| Confession | Witness |

Note
- This duty to continually review disclosure material applies both AFTER conviction and pending APPEAL.

1st Description
- Applies to the alleged offender.

Explanation
- Of the alleged offender for the offence.

Confession
- Any material casting doubt on the reliability of a confession.

Witness
- Any material casting doubt on the reliability of the witness.

WHETHER OR NOT IT UNDERMINES THE PROSECUTION CASE

Additional Key Phrases

OIC, Investigator, Disclosure Officer

⬇

Separate roles, however, dependent on the complexity of the case may be combined

The Prosecutor is responsible for ensuring Initial and Secondary disclosure is presented to the Defence i.e. not the OIC, Investigator or Disclosure Officer

Conflict of Interest for DO?

| Advice of a more Senior Officer MUST be sought | If still in doubt, the advice of the prosecutor SHOULD be sought |

Note
- The Disclosure Officer can be a member of Police Staff so not just an Officer and includes Deputies.

Observation Posts

A police officer not below the rank of

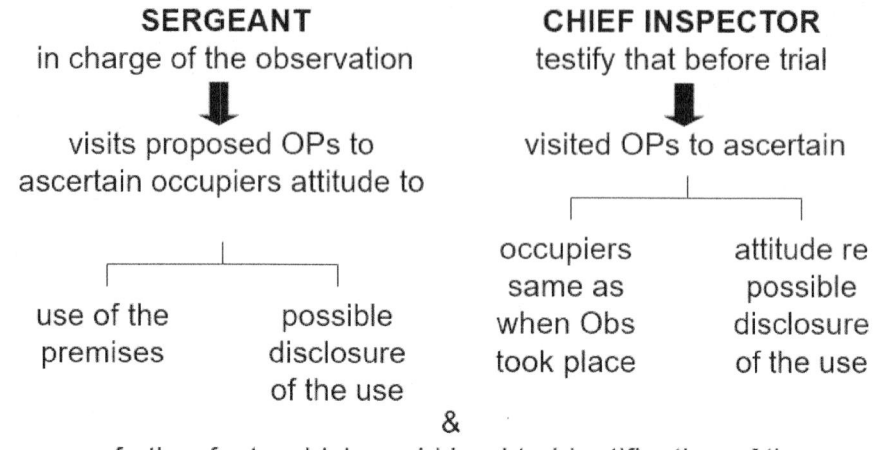

SERGEANT	**CHIEF INSPECTOR**
in charge of the observation	testify that before trial
↓	↓
visits proposed OPs to ascertain occupiers attitude to	visited OPs to ascertain

| use of the premises | possible disclosure of the use | occupiers same as when Obs took place | attitude re possible disclosure of the use |

&

of other facts which could lead to identification of the premises AND occupiers

R v Johnson (1988)
- These are the minimum evidential requirements needed if disclosure of the OP is to be protected.
- Such evidence will be given in the absence of the jury.

Blake v DPP (1993)
- These guidelines do not require a threat of violence before such protection can be afforded to the occupier of an OP – it suffices if the occupier is in fear of harassment.

R v Brown & Daley (1987)
- This is based on the protection of the owner or occupier and NOT the identity of the premises itself. So, where officers have witnessed the commission of the offence from an unmarked police vehicle, information relating to the surveillance, make and model of the car could not be withheld.

Retention Periods for Material

Material must be retained until a decision is taken to

| prosecute | and then until the case has been dealt with |

In the event of a conviction it must be retained at least until

| release from custody | otherwise 6 months after conviction |

In the case of an Appeal, until conclusion or failure to proceed

Q. If the OIC believes that other persons may be in possession of material relevant to the investigation what should the OIC do?
A. Ask the Disclosure officer to inform them and invite them to retain the material in case they receive a request from the disclosure.

Q. Who should inform the Prosecutor?
A. Disclosure officer.

QUESTION

Where a person is due in court for speeding and there is video evidence, how long should the recording be retained?

A. Up until the person has been convicted.
B. Up until the end of any enforcement period.

Answer B.

On the basis that the driver may decide to contest the decision once convicted

QUESTION

Where there is a possibility of CCTV footage relating to an offence, are the police under any obligation to seize and retain such material?

A. Yes, all such CCTV footage will be seized and retained.
B. No, CCTV footage does not have to be retained in all cases.

Answer B.
However, it very much depends on the circumstances, so read the question carefully to determine whether the police have a clear duty to seize such material for example, in R v Dobson (2001), potential CCTV was available which MAY have exonerated the defendant on the basis he was elsewhere at the time of the offence for which he was later convicted.

Apparently, the defence didn't ask for the tapes to be preserved during interview while the possibility for reviewing the tapes was overlooked and were overwritten after 31 days.

Luckily for the prosecution the obvious prejudice to the defendant's case was not considered 'Serious' by the Court, partially because the defence had the opportunity to ask for them to be seized and preserved along with the fact that any such content may not have been conclusive on the part of the defence.

QUESTION

JONES was sentenced at court to a term of imprisonment of 18 months. However, owing to the length of time he had spent on remand and other factors, he was released after five months from the date of his conviction.

In relation to the retention of material as outlined by the Criminal Procedure and Investigations Act 1996, which of the following statements is correct?

A. The material no longer needs to be retained.
B. The material will need to be retained for a further 1 month.
C. The material will need to be retained for a further 6 months.
D. The material will need to be retained for a further 13 months.

Answer B.
Six (6) months after conviction. If the person is released earlier than 6 months from the date of conviction then the materials must be retained until at least six months from the date of conviction.

GENERAL PRINCIPLES
POLICE POWERS & PROCEDURES

SESSION 7

THE REGULATION OF INVESTIGATORY
POWERS ACT 2000

Directed Surveillance

Is surveillance which is Covert for the purposes of a specific

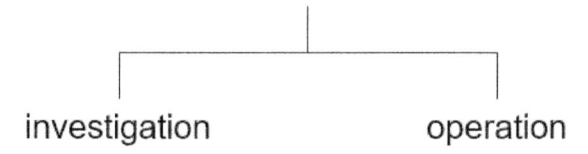

- investigation
- operation

likely to result in the obtaining of **private information** about **a person**

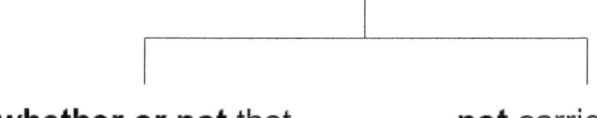

- **whether or not** that person has been **identified**
- **not** carried out **in immediate response** to events / circumstances

Private Information
- Relates to a person's private / family life including personal relationships which MAY extend to those of a professional or business nature.
- Whilst a person may have a reduced expectation of privacy when in a public place, covert surveillance of that person's activities in public may still result in the obtaining of *private information*.
- This is likely to be the case as that person has a reasonable expectation of privacy even though acting in public e.g. having a drink in the pub with a friend. Add to this the fact that a record of this conversation will be made, the requirement for 'directed surveillance' application / authorisation is likely to be required.
- It does NOT generally include use of CCTV or ANPR, but where CCTV is used to monitor a specific individual such as a person believed to be involved in drug dealing (think a County Lines type question perhaps), this would be considered covert and therefore require authorisation.

- Equally, prolonged surveillance targeted on a single person will undoubtedly result in the obtaining of private information about that person, but this can also apply to others with whom that person comes into contact, hence the term *a person* rather than just the person who is the subject of the surveillance.

Whether or not that person has been identified
- Clearly, not all investigations have a known suspect from the outset and as such whether one is talking about, for example, the following up of anonymous information that an unknown person to commit a robbery at the local post office then 'directed surveillance' may well be a tactical option for consideration.

Immediate Response
- Covert surveillance that is likely to reveal *private information* about a person, but when carried out by way of an immediate response to events in such a way that it is not reasonably practicable to obtain an authorisation, this would not require a directed surveillance authorisation for example, an off duty officer in a pub overhearing two persons discussing the robbery of the aforementioned post office.
- The fine line hear however, is at what point in time would this immediate response criteria no longer apply.
- Lets say, for example the officer calls in the information on his/her mobile phone and is subsequently joined by a colleague with a view to corroborate and/or perhaps record the conversation then clearly what we have now is an operation which has extended beyond the remit of 'immediate response' and will require 'directed surveillance' authorisation.

Intrusive Surveillance

Intrusive surveillance is covert surveillance that is carried out in relation to anything taking place

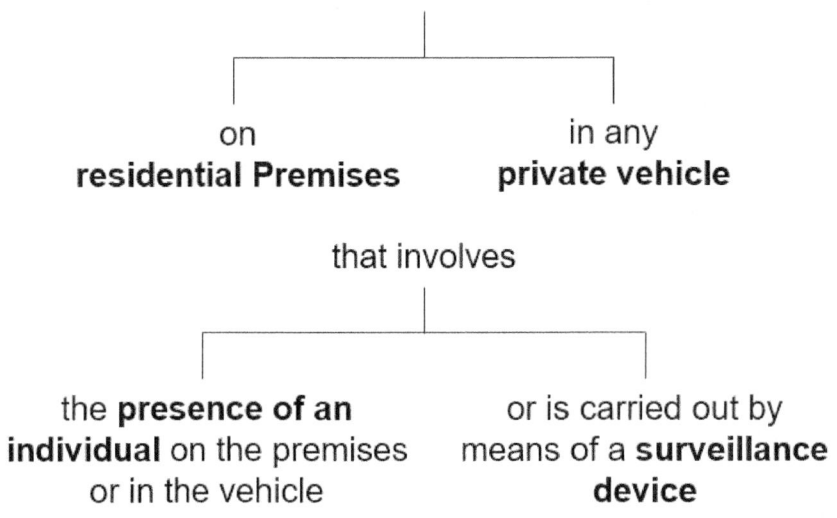

- on **residential Premises**
- in any **private vehicle**

that involves

- the **presence of an individual** on the premises or in the vehicle
- or is carried out by means of a **surveillance device**

Note
- Perhaps the most important factor missing from this definition when compared to the one for 'Directed Surveillance' is that 'Intrusive Surveillance' relates to the *location* of the surveillance.
- It is not therefore necessary to consider whether or not intrusive surveillance is likely to result in the obtaining of *private information* merely *where* and *how* it is taking place.

Residential premises
- Are considered to be so much of any premises as is for the time being occupied or used by any person, *however temporarily*, for residential purposes or otherwise as living accommodation.
- Includes vehicles or moveable structures whether or not occupied as land.

Q. With regard to residential premises, would this include hotel or prison accommodation that is so occupied or used?

A. Yes, however, common areas (such as hotel dining areas) to which a person has access in connection with their use or occupation of accommodation are specifically excluded.

Q. Under what circumstances could the placing of a covert surveillance device in ANY premises be considered intrusive?
A. Where legal consultations are taking place e.g. Prison, Police Station, Solicitors offices, Psychiatric hospitals etc.

Private vehicle
- Any vehicle and includes vessels, aircraft or hovercraft, which are *used primarily for the private purposes of the person who owns it or a person otherwise having the right to use it.* This would a company car, owned by a leasing company and used for business and pleasure by the employee of a company.

QUESTION

Having been arrested for aggravated burglary, false imprisonment and possession of a firearm off the back of a pre-planned operation, the GRADY brother's subsequent conversation in the back of a police van on route to the police station is covertly recorded.

Given these circumstances, in accordance with The Regulation of Investigatory Powers Act 2000, which of the following statements is correct?

A. The police van *will not* be regarded as a private vehicle and therefore this action represents 'Directed Surveillance,' subject to authorisation by a superintendent or above.
B. The police van *will* be regarded as a private vehicle and therefore this action represents 'Intrusive Surveillance,' subject to authorisation by a Chief Constable or Commissioner.

Answer A.

Q. When considering the issue of private vehicles, under what circumstances may this apply to a Hackney Carriage or Private Hire Taxi?
A. This would only apply when NOT being used as a Taxi and therefore as a private vehicle.

Note
- Surveillance is not intrusive if carried out using only a surveillance device designed or adapted for the purpose of providing information about the location of the vehicle e.g. a vehicle tracker.

Presence of an individual / Surveillance Device
- Intrusive surveillance may take place by means of a person or device located in the residential premises or private vehicle.

Q. When considering the use of a surveillance device outside a residential premises or private vehicle what criteria is required for this to constitute Intrusive Surveillance?
A. The information is consistently of the same quality and detail as might be obtained from a device in the premises.

DIRECTED	INTRUSIVE

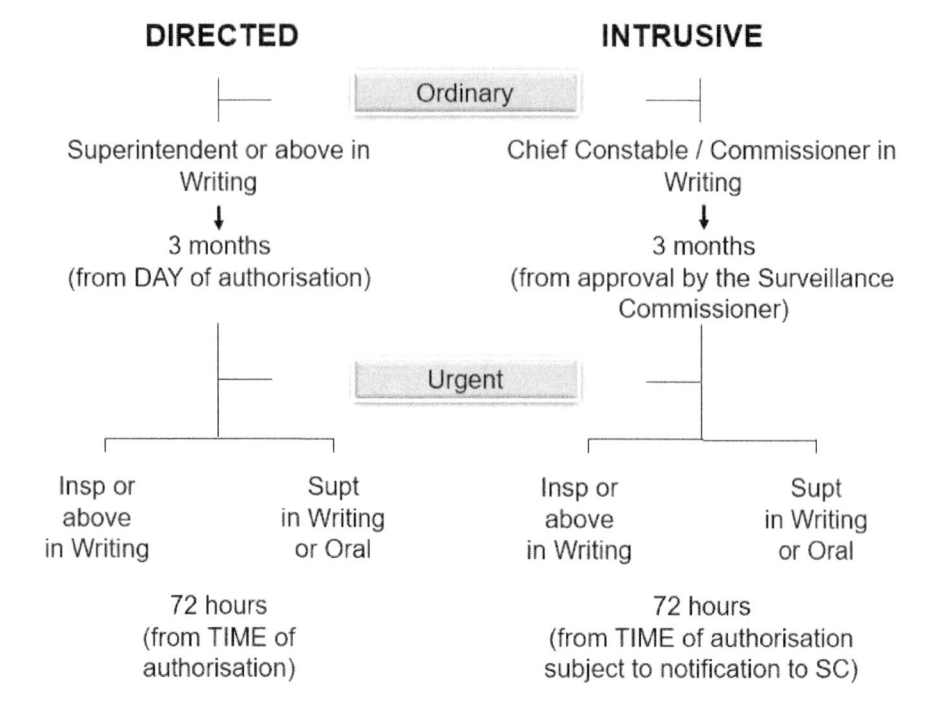

Ordinary

Superintendent or above in Writing	Chief Constable / Commissioner in Writing
↓	↓
3 months (from DAY of authorisation)	3 months (from approval by the Surveillance Commissioner)

Urgent

Insp or above in Writing	Supt in Writing or Oral	Insp or above in Writing	Supt in Writing or Oral
72 hours (from TIME of authorisation)		72 hours (from TIME of authorisation subject to notification to SC)	

Authorisation Criteria

- In each instance relevant officers must BELIEVE the authorisation is BOTH necessary and proportionate based on specific grounds:
    - Directed
        - Interests of national security;
        - Preventing or detecting crime or preventing disorder;
        - Economic well-being of UK;
        - Public safety;
        - Protecting public health;
        - Assessing, collecting tax etc.
    - Intrusive
        - Interest of national security;
        - Preventing or detecting SERIOUS crime;
        - Economic well-being of the UK.

Note

- Preventing or detecting crime applies in both cases HOWEVER *preventing disorder* only applies to Directed while *serious crime* only applies to Intrusive.

Covert Human Intelligence Source

A person is a CHIS if he/she **establishes or maintains** a **personal or other relationship** with a person for the covert purpose of

| using such a relationship to **obtain information** or to **provide access to any** information to another person | **disclosing information** obtained by the use of such a relationship or as a consequence of the existence of such a relationship. |

Note
- The obtaining of private information is not relevant where CHISs are concerned.
- This is all about the covert manipulation of a relationship to gain any information. Accordingly, any manipulation of a relationship by the police is likely to engage Article 8 HRA, regardless of whether or not the police intends to acquire private information.
- It doesn't normally apply to those people who might otherwise be expected to pass on information to the police e.g. local authority, banks.

HOWEVER

- If having received information, the police task the person to delve deeper in order to develop the information, this could then fall within this category.

Covert Human Intelligence Sources
Authorisations

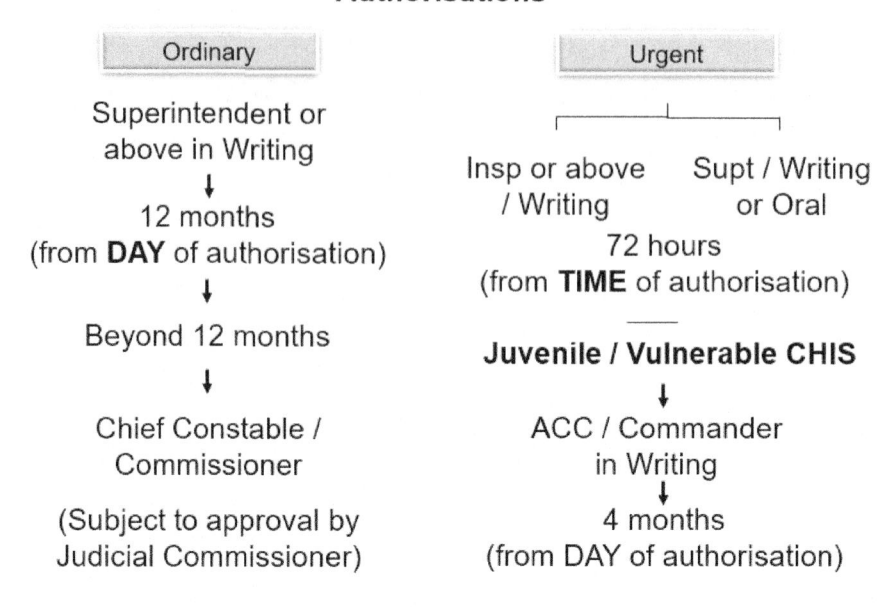

Ordinary

Superintendent or above in Writing
↓
12 months
(from **DAY** of authorisation)
↓
Beyond 12 months
↓
Chief Constable / Commissioner

(Subject to approval by Judicial Commissioner)

Urgent

Insp or above / Writing   Supt / Writing or Oral

72 hours
(from **TIME** of authorisation)

Juvenile / Vulnerable CHIS
↓
ACC / Commander in Writing
↓
4 months
(from DAY of authorisation)

Note
- Authorising officers SHOULD so NOT MUST, where possible be independent of the investigation.

Undercover Officers aka Relevant Sources
- ACC / Commander in writing / 12 months.

U16
- Not allowed to INFORM on their parents or those with parental responsibility.

GENERAL PRINCIPLES
POLICE POWERS & PROCEDURES

SESSION 8

COURT PROCEDURE AND WITNESSES

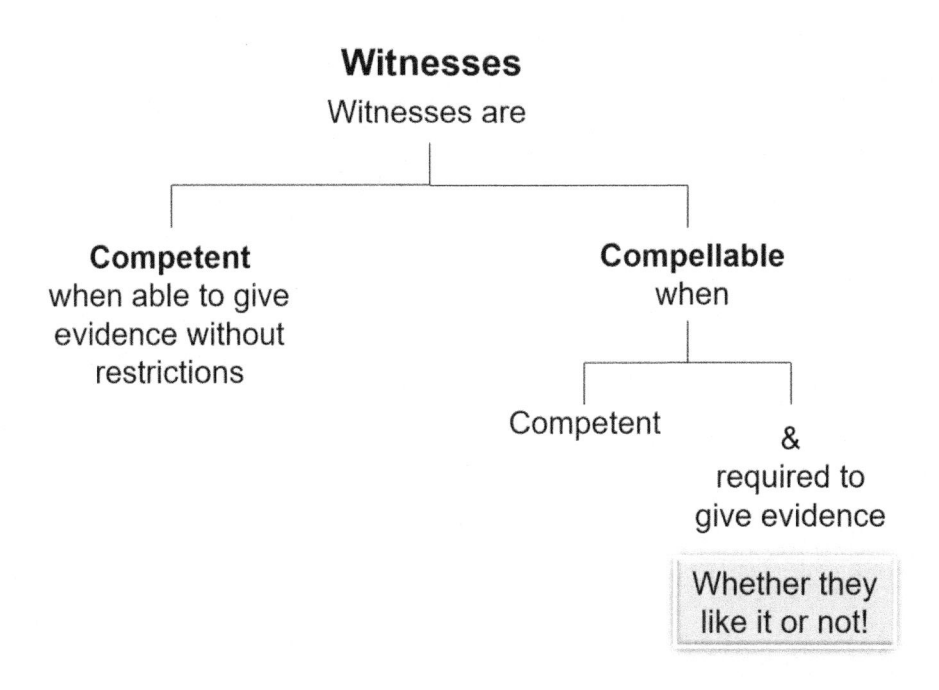

Witnesses

Witnesses are

Competent
when able to give evidence without restrictions

Compellable
when

Competent & required to give evidence

> Whether they like it or not!

Q. Is an accused COMPETENT to give evidence against a co-accused?

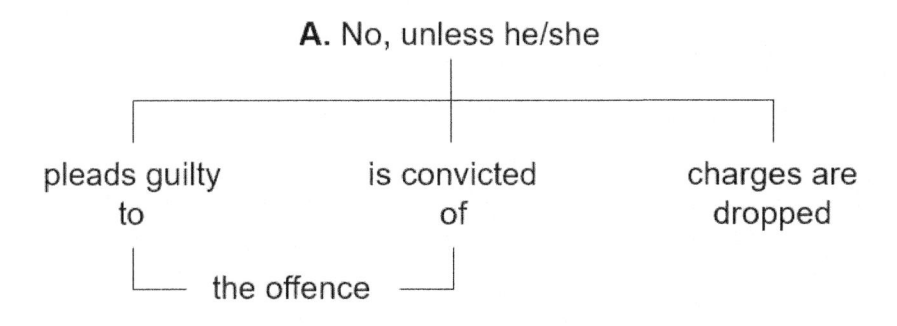

A. No, unless he/she

- pleads guilty to
- is convicted of
- charges are dropped

└── the offence ──┘

Q. What if the accused suggests in evidence that they did not take part in the offence?

A. Unless the plea is set aside, they remain competent.

Accused / Spouses / Civil Partners

A person CANNOT be compelled to give evidence against a spouse or civil partner charged with an offence unless

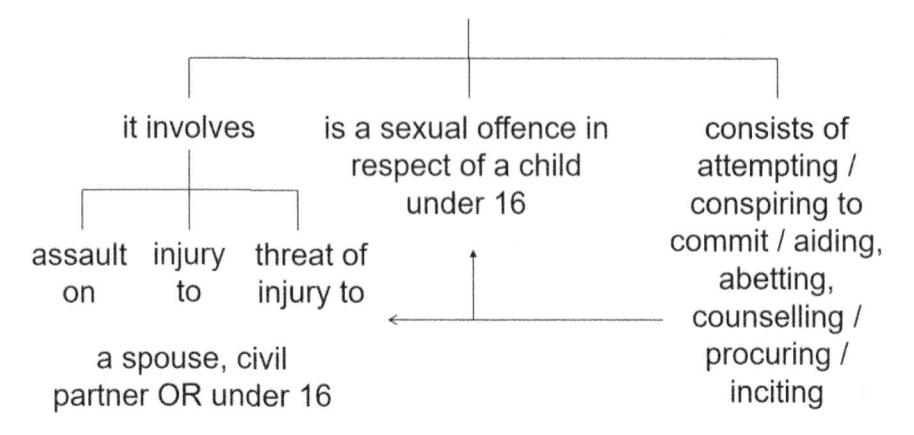

- **it involves**
  - assault on
  - injury to
  - threat of injury to

  a spouse, civil partner OR under 16

- **is a sexual offence in respect of a child under 16**

- **consists of attempting / conspiring to commit / aiding, abetting, counselling / procuring / inciting**

Under 16
- At the material time, so at the time of the offence.

Extends to
- Same sex couples.
- Opposite sex couples.
- But NOT Co-habitees.

Q. Is there a requirement to inform a wife that she is NOT compellable to give evidence against her husband prior to interview?
A. No, even if the wife subsequently refused to give evidence however, the case would be strengthened if she had been so informed prior to the interview.

Q. What if a person is no longer married or in a relevant relationship with the accused?
A. They are compellable.

Child Witnesses

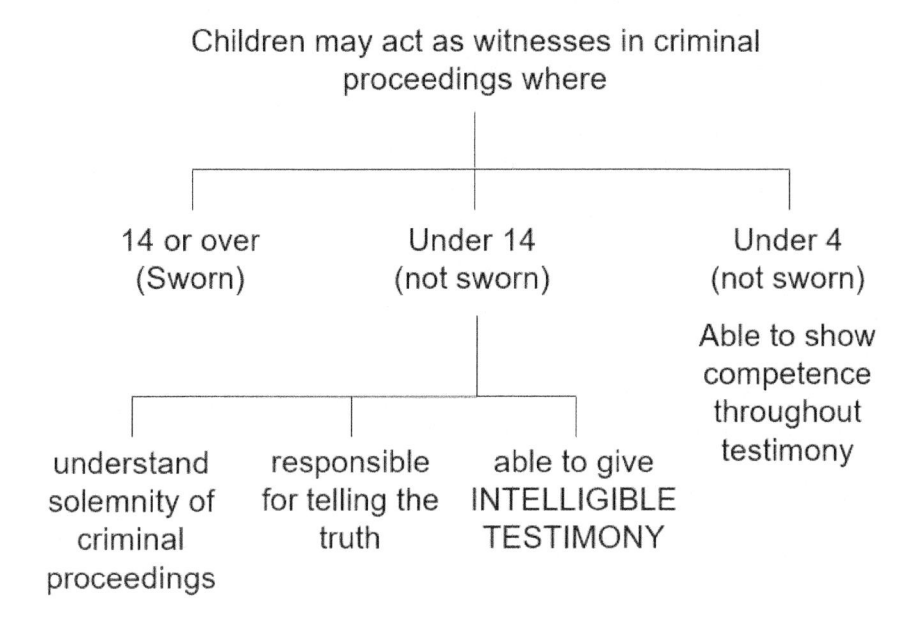

Children may act as witnesses in criminal proceedings where

- **14 or over (Sworn)**
  - understand solemnity of criminal proceedings
  - responsible for telling the truth
- **Under 14 (not sworn)**
  - responsible for telling the truth
  - able to give INTELLIGIBLE TESTIMONY
- **Under 4 (not sworn)**
  - Able to show competence throughout testimony

Intelligible Testimony
- Determined by either 'Expert Testimony' or where the court decides the Witness.
- Understands questions.
- Is able to provide answers which can be understood.
- Also applies to persons with a mental disability of the mind e.g. Alzheimer's / psychiatric condition

Q. Where the age of ANY person is pertinent to the proceedings, what is required where a birth certificate has been presented as proof of age?
A. Supporting evidence to identify the person AS THE person on the certificate.

Q. What happens if a statement made by an accused as to his/her age conflicts with that of the appearance of the individual?
A. The statement of the accused may be disregarded.

Birth Certificates
- Reference is also made to a statement made by a person present at the birth of the individual being useful in difficult cases however, base on this wording it could not be considered as proof.

Witness Anonymity

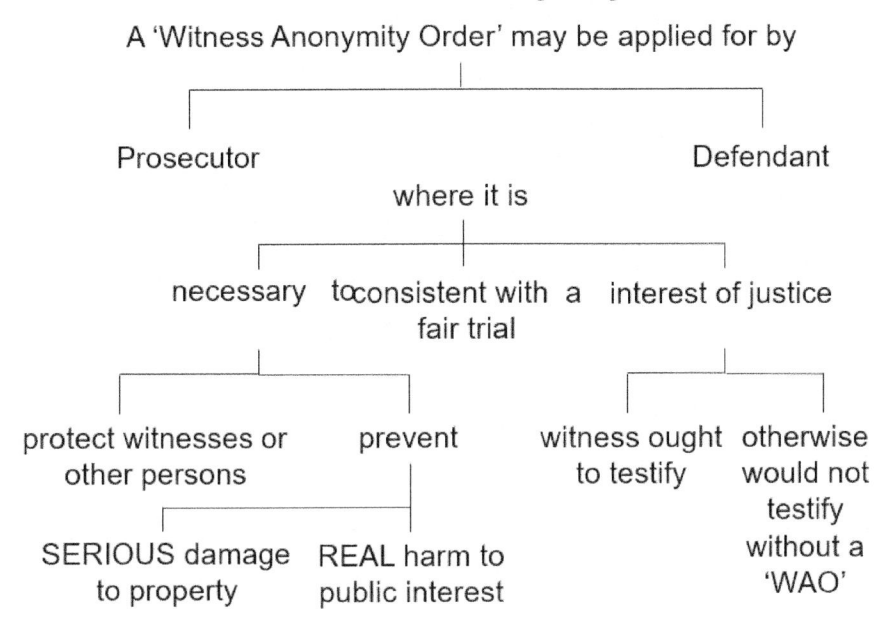

A 'Witness Anonymity Order' may be applied for by

- Prosecutor
- Defendant

where it is
- necessary
- consistent with a fair trial
- interest of justice

- protect witnesses or other persons
- prevent
  - SERIOUS damage to property
  - REAL harm to public interest
- witness ought to testify
- otherwise would not testify without a 'WAO'

QUESTION

Where TV live link witness testimony is approved, can this provision extend to telephones?

A. Yes, subject to the Court obtaining consent from both parties.
B. No, the Court has no power to authorise the use of a telephone, even with the consent of both parties.

Answer B.

QUESTION

At which of the following Court proceedings may TV live link be used for a witness outside the UK?

A. Trials on indictment, proceedings in youth court, appeals from Youth / Crown Court and extradition proceedings.

B. Trials on indictment, appeals from Crown Court and extradition proceedings.

Answer A.

Q. For the purposes of refreshing memory, a document, including a tape recording is regarded as anything in which information of any description is recorded except?
A. Recording of sounds of moving images.

QUESTION

In which of the following circumstances are witnesses entitled to view a video recording of their interview to refresh their memories?

A. At any time before trial including immediately before giving evidence.
B. At any time before trial excluding immediately before giving evidence.

Answer B.

QUESTION

When considering the issue of 'confessions' as defined by s.82 PACE 1984, which of the following statements is correct?

A. Where a confession is excluded, other evidence, perhaps from the interview process, and not affected by the confession *may not* necessarily be excluded.
B. Where a confession is excluded, other evidence, perhaps from the interview process, and not affected by the confession *will also* be excluded.

Answer A. Where a confession is excluded, other evidence, perhaps from the interview process, and not affected by the confession *may not* necessarily be excluded, *but may impact on its value.*

Printed in Great Britain
by Amazon